GCSE English

An Inspector Calls

by J.B. Priestley

Studying English texts can give you a real headache,
but happily this CGP book makes your life just a little bit easier.

This book has everything you need to write a brilliant essay about *An Inspector Calls*.
It doesn't just tell you what happens — it's got analysis of the main characters,
themes, historical background and language features too.

Plus, there are plenty of practice questions and a worked exam answer
with tips on how to improve your grade on the big day.

And of course, we've done our best to make the whole
experience at least vaguely entertaining for you.

The Text Guide

Foundation Level

Introduction

Section One — Discussion of Acts

Section Two — Characters

Contents

Section Three — Themes

Section Four — The Writer's Techniques

Section Five — Assessment Advice

Published by CGP

Editors:
David Broadbent
Luke von Kotze
Anthony Muller
Holly Poynton

Contributor:
Peter Needham

With thanks to Rebecca Tate and Nicola Woodfin for the proofreading.
With thanks to Laura Jakubowski for the copyright research.

With thanks to:

Cover photograph by Rubén Hidalgo with kind permission of iStockphoto.com

Photos of An Inspector Calls at Lamb's Players Theatre, Coronado, California / directed by Robert Smyth / cast: Glynn Bedington, Jilian Frost, David Cochran Heath, Jon Lorenz, Colleen Kollar Smith. Lance Arthur Smith, Robert Smyth / photos by Ken Jacques and Nathan Peirson

With thanks to Mary Evans Picture Library for permission to use the images on pages 1, 2 & 34

With thanks to Getty Images for permission to use the images on pages 1 & 37

With thanks to iStockphoto.com for permission to use the images on pages 3, 4 & 30

With thanks to Donald Cooper/photostage.co.uk for permission to use the images on pages 3, 7, 11 & 29

With thanks to Simon Gough Photography for permission to use the images on pages 3, 5, 6, 9, 10, 12, 13, 20, 23, 24, 26, 27, 28, 40, 41 & 47

With thanks to TopFoto.co.uk for permission to use the images on pages 3 & 5

With thanks to Rex Features for permission to use the images on pages 3, 4, 11, 18, 19, 25, 45 & 46

Images on pages 8, 21 & 22 © WATERGATE PRODS / THE KOBAL COLLECTION

Extract on pg 52 from An Inspector Calls and other plays by J.B.Priestley, published by Penguin Books 1969, Penguin Classics 2000. 'An Inspector Calls' copyright 1947 by J.B.Priestley. Reproduced by permission of Penguin Books Ltd

ISBN: 978 1 84762 903 6

Website: www.cgpbooks.co.uk

Printed by Elanders Ltd, Newcastle upon Tyne.

Clipart from CorelDRAW®

Based on the classic CGP style created by Richard Parsons.

Introduction to 'An Inspector Calls' and J.B. Priestley

'An Inspector Calls' is about how **unfair society** can be

- *An Inspector Calls* is a play about a rich family who are accused of being responsible for the suicide of a young working-class girl.
- J.B. Priestley wrote the play in 1945, but it is set in 1912.
- In 1912, the rich middle class and upper class had more power than the working class.
- Priestley wanted people in 1945 to think about how unfair society was.

An Inspector Calls has a strong message...

1) The play is set just before the start of the First World War. The war began in 1914 and killed millions of people. The characters' world is about to face a terrible disaster.
2) Priestley set the play in 1912 to warn his audience that they might have a similar disaster if they didn't learn from past mistakes.

A soldier receives first aid in 1916, during the First World War.

The **Second World War** influenced J. B. Priestley

- *An Inspector Calls* was written near the end of the Second World War. Soldiers were returning from the war and hoping for a better life.
- Priestley wanted his audience to realise that everybody must work together to improve society.

1894	Born in Bradford
1914-18	First World War. Priestley was wounded but survived.
1919-21	Studied at Cambridge University.
1939	Second World War starts.
1941-42	Priestley wanted a more equal society. He set up some socialist organisations to try to achieve this.
1945	Second World War ends. First performance of 'An Inspector Calls'.
1984	Died, aged 89.

For more about socialism, see p.38.

Background Information

The play's set in **Brumley**

Brumley is made-up, but it's based on real cities in the Midlands. In 1912, cities like this were full of factories and thousands of factory workers. Here are the key locations in the play:

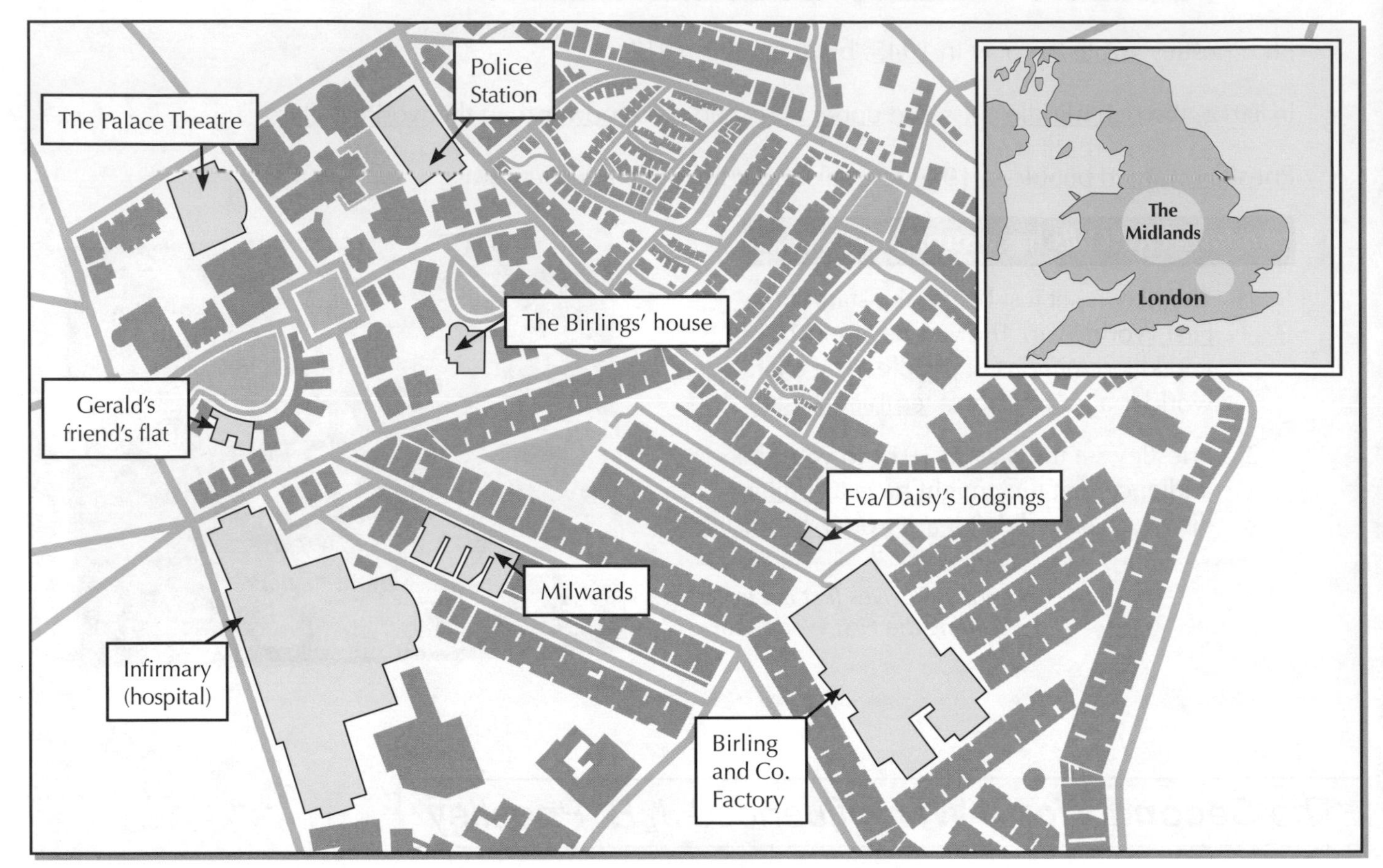

The **upper classes** were **rich** and the **working classes** were **poor**

Women working in a carpet factory in 1902.

- In 1912 the upper and middle classes were rich and powerful because they had money and good jobs.
- The working class had to work hard for not much money, often in factories owned by the middle class.
- People were expected to look after themselves, so there wasn't much help for poor people who were having a hard time.

Who's Who in Brumley

Arthur Birling...

... is a rich businessman who owns a factory. He's in charge of his family.

Sybil Birling...

... is Arthur's wife. She's snobby and obsessed with social class.

Eric Birling...

... is the Birlings' son. He's a secret alcoholic who's going to inherit his father's business.

Gerald Croft...

... is an upper-class businessman. He's about thirty, and is engaged to Sheila.

Sheila Birling...

... is the Birlings' daughter. She's in her early twenties, and is engaged to Gerald.

Edna...

... is the Birlings' maid. She's the only working-class woman on stage.

The Inspector...

... is a mysterious man who claims to be a police inspector. He's investigating the death of Eva/Daisy.

Eva Smith/ Daisy Renton...

... is the victim of the play. The audience never see her on stage.

'An Inspector Calls' — Plot Summary

'An Inspector Calls'... what happens when?

Here are the main events of *An Inspector Calls*. It's a good idea to learn what happens when, so that you know how everything fits together.

Act One — one evening in 1912...

The Birlings celebrate Gerald and Sheila's engagement.

- The Birlings are a rich middle-class family. They are celebrating Sheila and Gerald's engagement.
- Inspector Goole arrives and says that a woman called Eva Smith has committed suicide. He starts to question the family.
- It turns out that Arthur Birling sacked Eva Smith from his factory for going on strike. Sheila then got Eva sacked from her next job at a shop.
- The Inspector says that Eva Smith changed her name to Daisy Renton. Gerald looks shocked and Eric leaves.

Act Two — everyone's involved with Eva/Daisy's death

- Gerald confesses he had an affair with Daisy Renton.
- Sheila gives him back her engagement ring. He gets upset and leaves.
- Sybil confesses that she refused to help Eva/Daisy. Eva/Daisy was pregnant at the time.
- Sybil blames the father of Eva/Daisy's child for her death. Sheila guesses that Eric was the father.

Inspector Goole questions the Birlings.

Act Three — Eric brings **shame** on the **family**

- Eric comes back. He knows that everyone thinks he's the father of Eva/Daisy's child.
- He confesses that he forced her to have sex. He got her pregnant and then stole money to support her.
- Eva/Daisy rejected the stolen money and turned to Sybil's charity for help.
- The Inspector warns the Birlings that unless everyone learns to look after each other, there will be even more suffering.
- The Inspector leaves the Birlings' house.

Birling is shocked by Eric's confession.

Act Three — the final **twist**...

The Inspector's visit upsets Sheila and Eric.

- Gerald returns and says he doesn't think the Inspector is who he is supposed to be.
- Birling calls the police and finds out there is no Inspector Goole. Gerald calls the hospital and finds out that no one has committed suicide. They all decide it's been a trick.
- The phone rings. A young woman has been found dead, and an Inspector is coming to question the Birlings...

Ring, ring — this is your future self calling...

...to say thanks for starting off your revision so well. Once you're sure you know what happens when in *An Inspector Calls*, turn over the page to start Section One. If you're still not 100% clear on the plot, turn to the back of the book for the cartoon...

Analysis of Act One — Arthur's Speech

The play starts with a party — the Birlings are celebrating Sheila and Gerald's engagement.

What happens in Act One

- The Birlings are having an engagement party when an inspector arrives.
- He tells them that a girl called Eva Smith has killed herself.
- It turns out that Birling sacked her from his factory, and then Sheila got her sacked from a shop.

*The Birlings seem like the **perfect family***

Each character plays their part:

- Arthur Birling is a successful businessman.
- Mrs Birling works hard to keep up the family's reputation.
- Eric works for Mr Birling in the family business.
- Sheila is engaged to Gerald Croft, the son of another successful businessman.

Sheila and Gerald celebrate their engagement.

*But **not everything** is OK*

1) Arthur Birling is nervous because Gerald's family are more successful and more important than he is.
2) Sheila's worried — she doesn't know what Gerald was up to last summer. She thinks he's lying when he says he was busy with work.

Birling** thinks he knows what will happen, but he's **wrong

1) Birling's sure that the future is bright — he gives a speech full of predictions about what lies ahead. But the audience of 1945 knows that he gets a lot of things wrong:

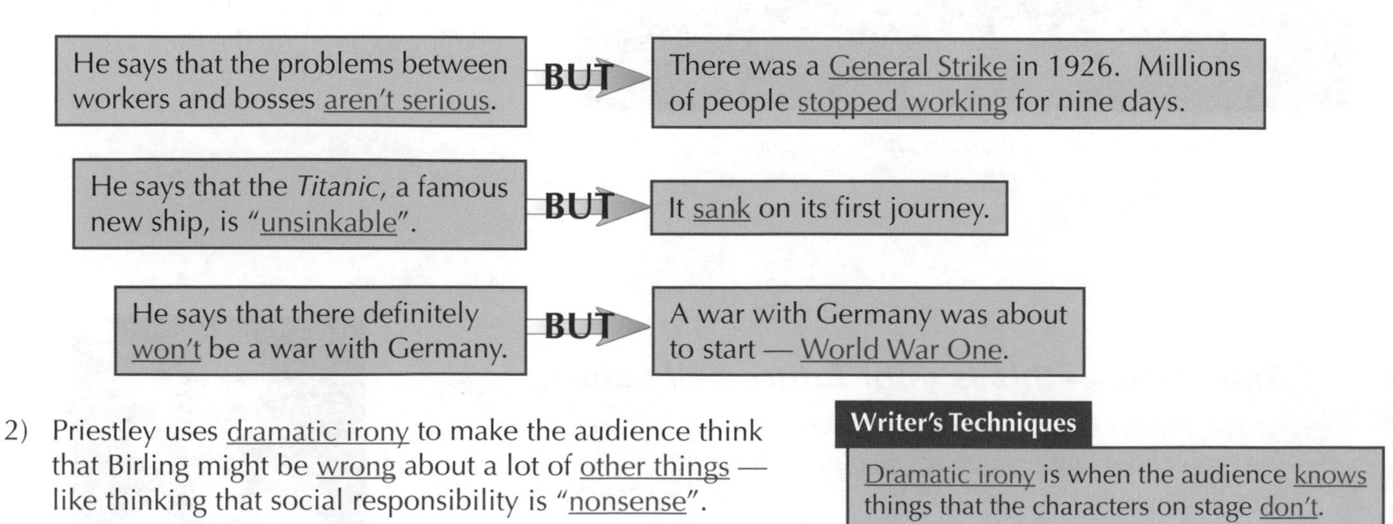

2) Priestley uses dramatic irony to make the audience think that Birling might be wrong about a lot of other things — like thinking that social responsibility is "nonsense".

Writer's Techniques

Dramatic irony is when the audience knows things that the characters on stage don't.

Analysis of Act One — The Inspector Begins

When the Inspector arrives, he begins to ask Mr Birling and Sheila about Eva Smith.

*An **Inspector** arrives and says a girl has **died***

1) The Inspector describes how a girl called Eva Smith has died. He uses harsh language — "Burnt her inside out". This contrasts with how polite and light-hearted the play seemed before he arrived.
2) The Inspector shows Birling a photo of Eva, but he doesn't let anyone else look at it.
3) This is important because the Inspector shows all the other characters the photo separately. He says it's the same photo, but the family later realise they might have been photos of different women.

*Birling **sacked** Eva Smith to protect his **business***

1) Birling explains that the workers at his factory went on strike because he wouldn't pay them any more money. The strike failed.
2) Birling sacked the strike's leaders, including Eva, to stop any more strikes.
3) This shows how much power the factory owners had over the working class.

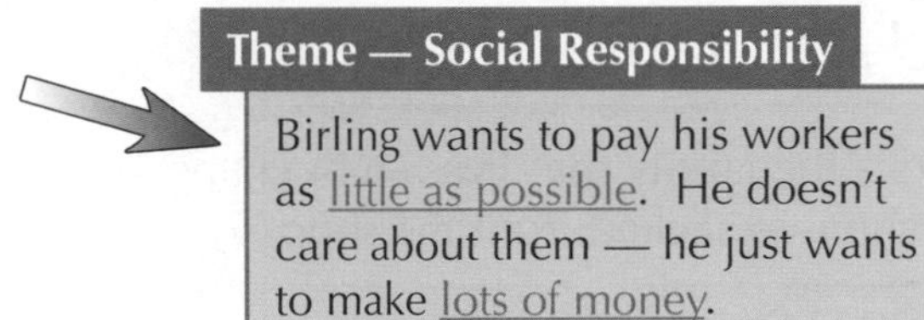

Theme — Social Responsibility

Birling wants to pay his workers as little as possible. He doesn't care about them — he just wants to make lots of money.

*Then **Sheila** got **Eva sacked** from her next job*

Sheila feels guilty for getting Eva sacked.

1) The Inspector shows Sheila a photo — it's a woman she got sacked from a shop last year.

Sheila had tried on a dress, and got jealous when she realised it would suit Eva (the shop assistant) better.

She was angry because Eva was pretty, and she thought Eva was laughing at her.

As an important customer she used her power to get Eva Smith sacked.

2) Sheila feels ashamed about how she acted. This shows she's grown up a bit since then. The audience might feel sorry for Sheila.

The Inspector tried to call — but they were engaged...

It all seemed to be going so well... The play quickly takes a bad turn when the doorbell rings. Priestley sets things up nicely for the arrival of the Inspector — things can't get any better, so they have to get worse.

Analysis of Act One — Eva Smith is Daisy Renton

The family starts to argue about Eva. The Inspector tells them that she changed her name to Daisy Renton.

Sheila and Eric **feel guilty** about what's happened

1) Eric says it was unfair to sack Eva Smith for asking for higher wages, when Birling's company tries to get the "highest possible prices" for the things they sell.
2) Eric and Sheila seem upset by the Inspector's story, but their parents don't seem to care.
3) Sheila's parents keep telling her to leave the room, but she stays because she feels it's her duty to hear the whole story.

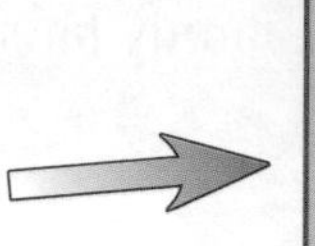

Theme — Young and Old

The Birlings don't think a young woman like Sheila should hear this horrible story, but Sheila is starting to think for herself.

Eva changed her name to **Daisy**

1) The Inspector tells the family that Eva Smith changed her name after she was sacked from the shop.

- Eva Smith could have changed her name to escape her past.
- Or maybe the Inspector is making up a story to link two separate women.

2) It's clear that Gerald knows who Daisy Renton is — he's "*startled*" when he hears the name.

Gerald is shocked when he hears Daisy's name.

Gerald **confesses** to Sheila

Theme — Men and Women

It was acceptable for men to have affairs, but it was unacceptable for women.

1) Birling and the Inspector leave to find Eric. Sheila and Gerald are left alone.
2) Sheila asks Gerald how he knows Daisy Renton. Gerald admits he had an affair with Daisy, but it was finished by the end of last summer.
3) Gerald tells Sheila not to tell the Inspector about his affair with Daisy. Sheila's sure that the Inspector knows about it already and she's worried about what else the Inspector might know.
4) When the Inspector comes back at the end of the Act he only says one word — "Well?". This shows that he knows Gerald has something to confess.

Analysis of Act Two — Gerald's Affair

Act Two starts with the Inspector questioning Gerald about how he came to know Daisy.

What happens in Act Two

- Gerald confesses that he had an affair with Eva/Daisy.
- He gave her money and a place to live for a while, but then he ended the affair.
- Sybil reveals that she refused to let her charity help Eva/Daisy, who was poor and pregnant.

*Gerald kept Daisy as his **mistress***

1) Gerald tries to get Sheila to leave the room so she doesn't hear any more details about his affair.
2) The Inspector points out that Gerald is a hypocrite — Gerald thinks Sheila should be "protected" because she's a young woman, but really Daisy Renton needed to be protected from him.
3) Gerald confesses to the affair. He isn't ashamed of what happened, "it wasn't disgusting", but Mrs Birling is shocked.

A hypocrite is someone who says one thing but then does the opposite.

*Daisy fell in **love** with **Gerald***

1) Gerald helped Daisy get away from a drunk man at a bar. They ended up having an affair — he gave her money and found her a place to live.
2) Gerald doesn't say he loved Daisy, but admits that he "adored" being loved by her. It's clear that there are good and bad things about the way Gerald treated Eva/Daisy:

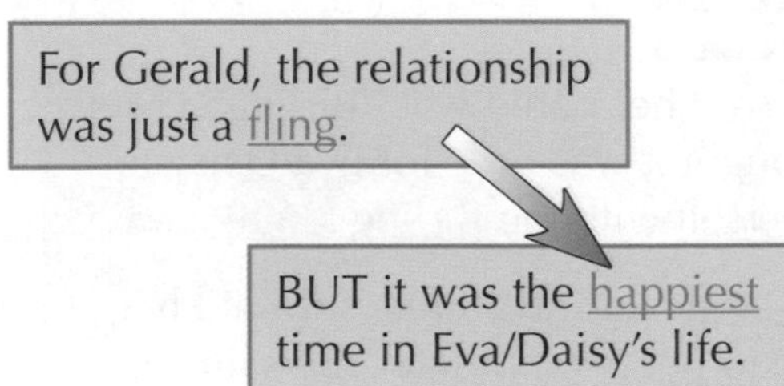

When they broke up, Gerald gave her some money.

BUT she had to move out of the flat he'd found for her — he made her homeless.

*Sheila **breaks off** the **engagement***

1) Gerald's confession proves that he's been lying to Sheila for months.
2) Sheila decides to end the engagement, as she feels like she doesn't really know Gerald any more.
3) Birling defends Gerald's behaviour because lots of men have mistresses.

Sheila breaks off her engagement with Gerald.

An animal like Gerald will never change his spots — he's such a cheetah...

Gerald's not used to people like the Inspector — he's blunt, rude and forceful. The Inspector's forceful approach works though — it keeps the plot moving and gets people to confess.

Analysis of Act Two — Sybil Refused to Help

The Inspector isn't done just yet — Sybil is the next family member to face the music.

Sybil Birling **won't admit** what she's done

1) The Inspector shows Sybil the photograph. She pretends she doesn't recognise it.
2) Even when the Inspector manages to get the story out of her, Sybil won't accept responsibility for what she did.
3) Sybil cares so much about her social class and reputation that she can't imagine herself in a situation like Eva/Daisy's. Because she can't imagine it, she can't feel sorry for Eva/Daisy.

Theme — Young and Old

The Inspector increases the tension between the parents and children by using Sheila's help to get Sybil to tell the whole story.

Sybil pretends she doesn't recognise the girl in the photo.

Sybil had the **last chance** to help but she **refused**

Eva/Daisy refused help from the father of her child for noble reasons, but Mrs Birling refused Eva/Daisy help for petty reasons:

Eva/Daisy's reasons

- The father was "silly and wild".
- He drank too much.
- The money he gave her was stolen.
- He didn't love her.
- She didn't want to get the father into any more trouble.

Mrs Birling's reasons

- Eva/Daisy said her name was "Birling". Mrs Birling thought it was rude for Eva/Daisy to connect herself with the Birling family name.
- She changed her story. At first she said her husband had left her, but later she said she wasn't married. Mrs Birling didn't trust her.
- Mrs Birling didn't believe Eva/Daisy's story. She didn't think a working-class girl would turn down money, even if it was stolen.

Sybil won't take **responsibility**

1) Mrs Birling tries to blame the child's father instead of admitting that she's done something wrong.
2) She blames the father for getting involved with a girl from the working class.
3) She can't believe that any man from her social class would drink heavily or steal. She says the father should be punished.

Analysis of Act Two — Sybil Blames the Father

Sybil tries to blame the father of Eva/Daisy's child, but she doesn't realise that Eric's the father.

*Mrs Birling really puts her **foot** in it*

1) The Inspector doesn't stop Sybil when she blames the father. It's a trap — Sybil doesn't realise she's asking for her own son to be punished.
2) Sheila is the only one who understands that her family are all guilty. She guesses that Eric is the father of Eva/Daisy's child.

Sybil blames the father of Eva/Daisy's child.

*Sheila quickly **works out** what's **going on***

1) The audience can see that Sheila has changed a lot from how she was in Act One — she has grown up and become more responsible.
2) Sheila can be determined and stubborn like her parents. But while her parents are determined to resist the Inspector, Sheila's determined to find out the truth.
3) Sheila demands that everyone answers the Inspector's questions. She tells Birling not to interfere when he sticks up for Gerald.

Themes — Learning about Life

Sheila realises that she's changed. When she breaks off her engagement with Gerald she says that they aren't "the same people" any more.

Eric** returns to **face the music

Eric feels guilty about what he's done.

1) Eric walks in, looking "*pale*" and upset. It's as if he realises that everyone knows he is guilty.
2) Eric left the dining room in Act One, and went out of the house earlier in Act Two. He's always running away from his family and what they expect of him.
3) Act Two finishes with a cliffhanger. The audience is left wondering whether or not Eric was the father of Eva/Daisy's child.

You'd think that Sybil would know a lot about responsybility...

Sybil blames "the father" for getting Eva/Daisy into this mess in the first place — she's trying to move the blame away from her and the rest of the Birlings. Only problem is, she doesn't know that Eric's the daddy.

Analysis of Act Three — Eric Confesses

This is the Act where everything falls apart. It all begins with Eric's confession...

What happens in Act Three

- Eric admits that he got Eva/Daisy pregnant.
- The Inspector tells them that they are all responsible, and then he leaves.
- The Birlings begin to think the Inspector wasn't a real policeman. Then the phone rings...

*Eric **confesses***

1) Eric admits to everything. He's realised that everyone knows he's the father of Eva/Daisy's child.
2) He explains that he forced her to have sex with him, when he was drunk.
3) He feels sorry for what he did, but he's still very childish. He calls Eva/Daisy "a good sport", which seems uncaring given how badly he treated her.
4) Eric's parents think he's acted worse than Gerald. This is only because what Eric did could cause a scandal, unlike Gerald who kept his affair secret.

*Birling's **angry** with Eric*

1) Arthur Birling starts to take the situation seriously for the first time. His son stole money from the company to help support Eva/Daisy.
2) In the middle of Eric's story Arthur orders the women to leave, so they don't have to hear the details.
3) What Eric did shocks his parents. He almost had a child with a woman who was probably a prostitute, which would have brought shame on his family.

Eric confesses he stole money from his father.

*Sybil returns and brings Eric **bad news***

1) Sybil and Sheila return to the dining room because Sybil had to know what happened.
2) Eric's been away, so it's only now that he finds out that Sybil refused to help Eva/Daisy. He's really angry, and says she's always been a bad parent: "You don't understand anything. You never did."

Theme — Family Life

Sybil cares more about how people see her family than having a good relationship with her children.

Analysis of Act Three — The Inspector's Speech

The Inspector points the finger of blame at everyone. Then he leaves. Charming...

The Inspector has his **say**

1) The Inspector sums up how each person had a hand in Eva/Daisy's suicide:

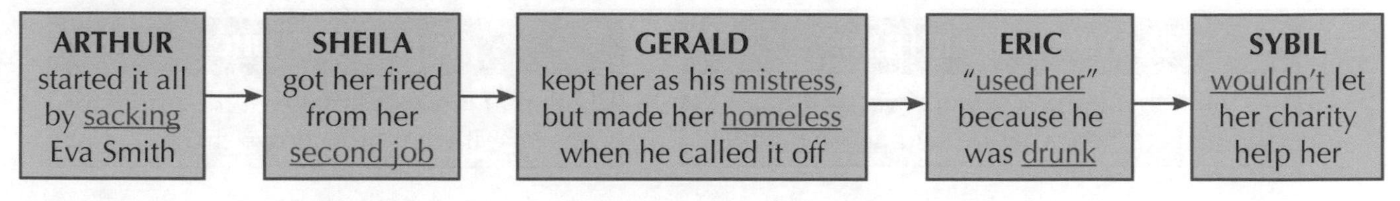

2) The Inspector gives a speech:

- He says that there are millions of people who are the same as Eva/Daisy. He thinks everyone should be responsible for everyone else, because everyone's affected by each other's actions.
- He warns that if people don't learn to look after each other, they'll be taught with "fire and blood and anguish".

The Birling family **falls apart**

1) After the Inspector leaves, Birling starts blaming Eric for their problems. The play goes straight from the Inspector's speech, to petty family rows.
2) They ignore the important message of the Inspector's speech and just go back to arguing about whose fault it is.
3) Birling doesn't want anything to change. He wants things to go back to how they were — with him in charge.

Birling blames Eric for everything.

Everyone's ashamed — but not everyone's **ashamed** of **themselves**

1) The Birling family say they're ashamed of each other.

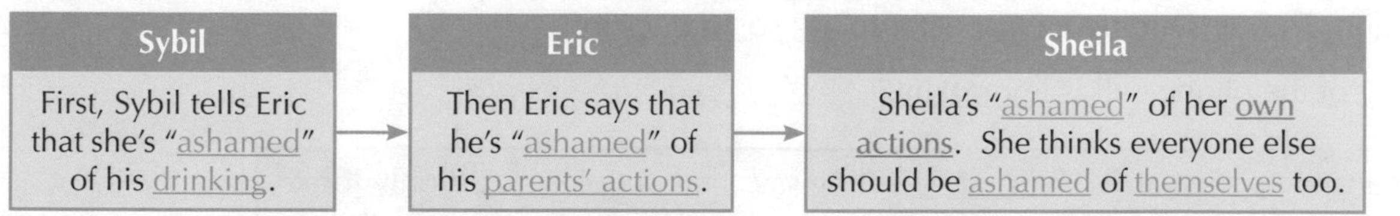

2) The parents haven't learnt anything. They care more about keeping everything secret. The only thing they'd really feel ashamed of is a scandal.
3) In contrast, Sheila and Eric think everyone should face up to their part in the tragedy.

I got the Inspector's message — he left it on the fridge...

The play's starting to come to a close — it's usually time for the main characters to learn their lessons. But this is the Birlings we're talking about. Some of them aren't going to learn anything. From anyone.

Analysis of Act Three — Was it a Trick?

Just when you think you've got it all worked out, there's a big twist. Turns out it was all a dream. Just kidding.

The Inspector might not have been a **real Inspector**

The Birlings think the Inspector might be a fake — but they have different ideas about how important that is:

SYBIL AND ARTHUR	SHEILA AND ERIC
think that if the Inspector wasn't a real policeman, then what he said doesn't matter.	think that it doesn't matter if the Inspector was fake if what he's shown them is true.

The family **checks** the **Inspector's story**

1) Gerald returns. He checked with a policeman — it turns out there's no Inspector Goole on the force.
2) Birling calls the police station. They tell him there is no Inspector Goole. Birling thinks it's all been a trick.
3) Gerald points out that they might have been shown photos of different girls.
4) Gerald calls the hospital — there hasn't been a suicide. Birling is relieved and he doesn't feel guilty anymore.
5) It's almost like a happy ending:

Photo: An Inspector Calls, ©2010 Lamb's Players Theatre

Birling calls the police station.

- Gerald and Mr and Mrs Birling relax and start joking about what's just happened. The atmosphere starts to seem like it did at the start of the play.
- Gerald suggests that he and Sheila should get engaged again. Sheila says it's "too soon" — she can't forget what she's learnt.

There's **another** phone call...

1) The police call to say that a girl has committed suicide by drinking disinfectant. They're sending an Inspector to ask some questions.
2) The timing of the phone call is important:

- The Inspector first arrived just after Birling says that people should only look after themselves. The Inspector's message was all about social responsibility.
- Birling laughs at Sheila and Gerald for taking the Inspector seriously. Then the phone rings — Birling hasn't learnt his lesson.

Maybe the Birlings should just unplug their phone...

The ending is very unsettling. Who was the Inspector? What would have happened if the Birlings had taken responsibility for their actions? Is the whole play a warning to the audience? Tune in next week to find out.

Practice Questions

So, how well do you know *An Inspector Calls* now...? Let's find out if you can pick out the important moments and details. Try answering these quick questions in a line or two.

Quick Questions

Act One

Q1 Give one reason why the Birlings seem like a 'perfect' family at the start of the play.

Q2 Name one prediction Birling gets wrong in his speech.

Q3 Why did Arthur Birling sack Eva Smith?

Q4 Why did Sheila Birling get Eva Smith sacked?

Act Two

Q5 Name one nice thing that Gerald did for Eva/Daisy.

Q6 What does Sheila do when she finds out that Gerald has had an affair?

Q7 Give one reason why Eva/Daisy refused help from her baby's father.

Q8 Who does Sybil say should be punished for Eva/Daisy's death?

Practice Questions

Want to feel like you're in the play? Pretend that I'm the Inspector and I'm giving you a good grilling. 'Ah hello. May I come in? I've got a few questions for you. Yes, it concerns a certain play...'

Quick Questions

Act Three

Q9 What piece of news makes Eric angry with his mother?

Q10 Name the three characters who don't learn anything from the Inspector.

Q11 Why does Gerald think Inspector Goole shows the photo to one character at a time?

Q12 What does the final phone call reveal?

This is where it gets a bit more serious. For these in-depth questions you need to write a paragraph or so.

In-depth Questions

Q1 Mrs Birling persuaded her charity not to help Eva/Daisy. In your own words, explain why she might have done this.

Q2 Do you think that Eva/Daisy's death is mostly one person's fault, or do you think that Gerald and the Birling family are all equally responsible? Give reasons for your answer.

Q3 Why do you think Priestley decided to have a twist at the end, instead of ending the play with the discovery that there was no suicide victim?

Character Profile — The Inspector

At the end of the play it's not clear who or what the Inspector was. Mr and Mrs Birling and Gerald want to know whether the Inspector was a fake, but Sheila and Eric think the Inspector's message is more important.

*The Inspector is in **charge***

1) The Inspector arrives near the beginning of the play. He says he wants to find out the truth about what happened to Eva/Daisy.
2) Unlike the Birlings, he doesn't seem to belong to a class. He isn't bothered about impressing them, so he's not worried about how he treats them.

Photo: An Inspector Calls, ©2010 Lamb's Players Theatre

Inspector Goole takes control of the room.

3) Although he's not a big man, he gets everyone's attention. He gives an impression of "massiveness, solidity and purposefulness".
4) He seems to know a lot about what's happened and what's about to happen.

Inspector Goole is...

Moral: "We are members of one body"

Controlling: "be quiet for a moment and listen to me"

Mysterious: "Was it a hoax?"

An outsider: "I thought I'd never seen you before"

*The Inspector isn't like the **other characters***

The Inspector doesn't behave like the Birlings:

- The Inspector doesn't play golf and he's not impressed by Arthur Birling's high profile as a former Alderman (council member) and Lord Mayor.
- He talks about subjects that are not meant to be talked about, like sex.
- He interrupts, repeats and pauses in unusual ways. He doesn't behave in the way that the middle classes would have expected.

*The Inspector is **classless***

1) The Inspector seems to come from outside the class system. This makes him 'classless'.
2) The Inspector doesn't agree with the Birlings' ideas about class. He treats everyone the same.
3) He says that "We are members of one body" which means that people should help each other.

Theme — Social Class

Priestley set his play in the Birlings' dining room. In 1912 only rich families had a dining room — this makes it a symbol of the middle class.

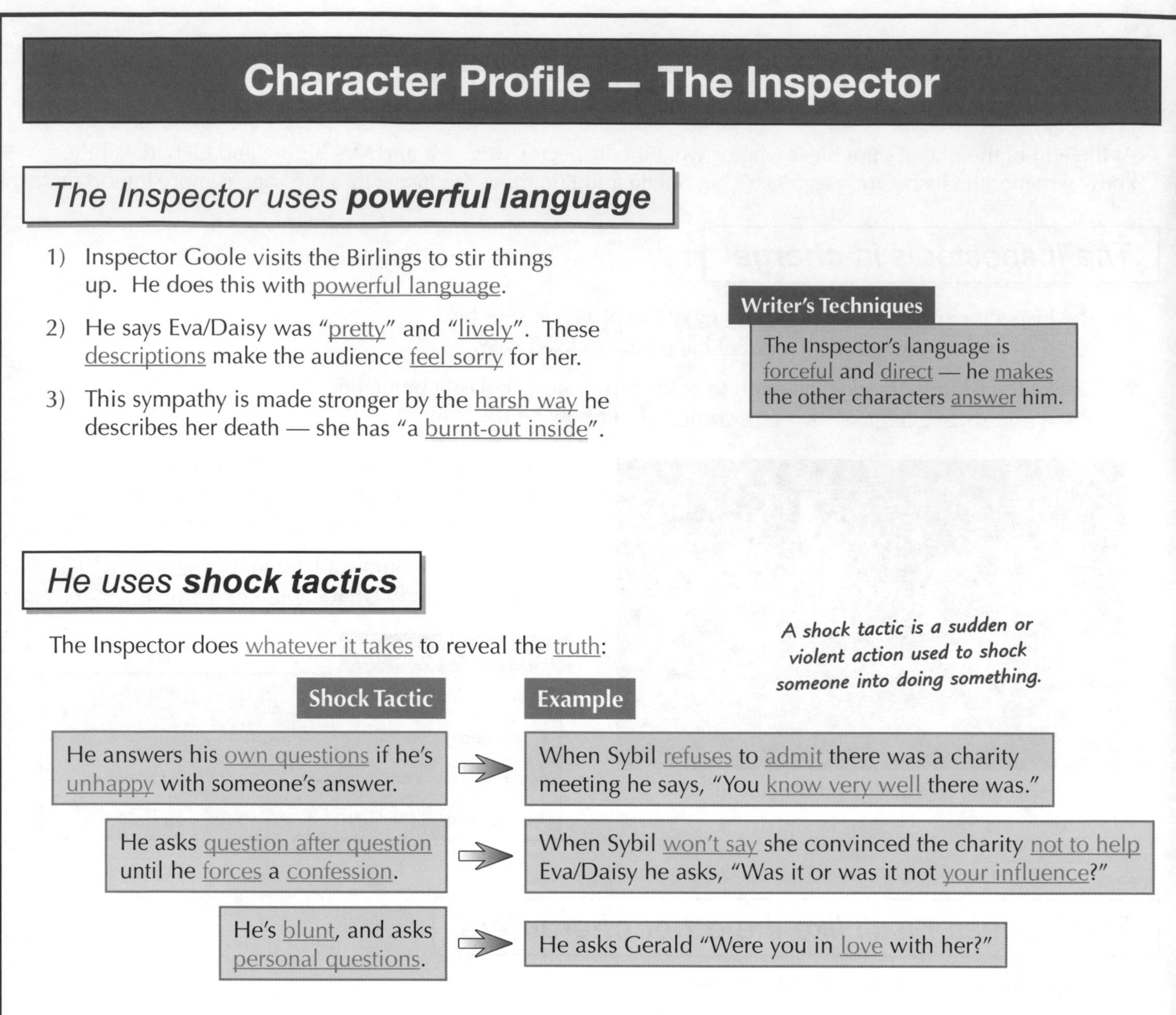

Character Profile — The Inspector

The Inspector uses **powerful language**

1) Inspector Goole visits the Birlings to stir things up. He does this with powerful language.
2) He says Eva/Daisy was "pretty" and "lively". These descriptions make the audience feel sorry for her.
3) This sympathy is made stronger by the harsh way he describes her death — she has "a burnt-out inside".

Writer's Techniques

The Inspector's language is forceful and direct — he makes the other characters answer him.

He uses **shock tactics**

The Inspector does whatever it takes to reveal the truth:

A shock tactic is a sudden or violent action used to shock someone into doing something.

Shock Tactic	Example
He answers his own questions if he's unhappy with someone's answer.	When Sybil refuses to admit there was a charity meeting he says, "You know very well there was."
He asks question after question until he forces a confession.	When Sybil won't say she convinced the charity not to help Eva/Daisy he asks, "Was it or was it not your influence?"
He's blunt, and asks personal questions.	He asks Gerald "Were you in love with her?"

His **authority** lets him keep **control**

© Donald Cooper/Rex Features

The Inspector is very confident.

1) The Inspector might just seem powerful because he's so confident. He knows how to unsettle people and make them do what he wants.
2) He controls the play's action, dealing with each character one at a time. The other characters get confused, but the Inspector never does.
3) He interrupts the other characters and even decides when they can speak e.g. when he tells Birling that Eric will "wait his turn".
4) His authority makes people take him seriously, and makes everything he says sound important.

Character Profile — The Inspector

Whooo is this Inspector Goole?

1) At the end of the play, the audience isn't sure who or what the Inspector is.
2) He seems to know everything but it's never properly explained how:

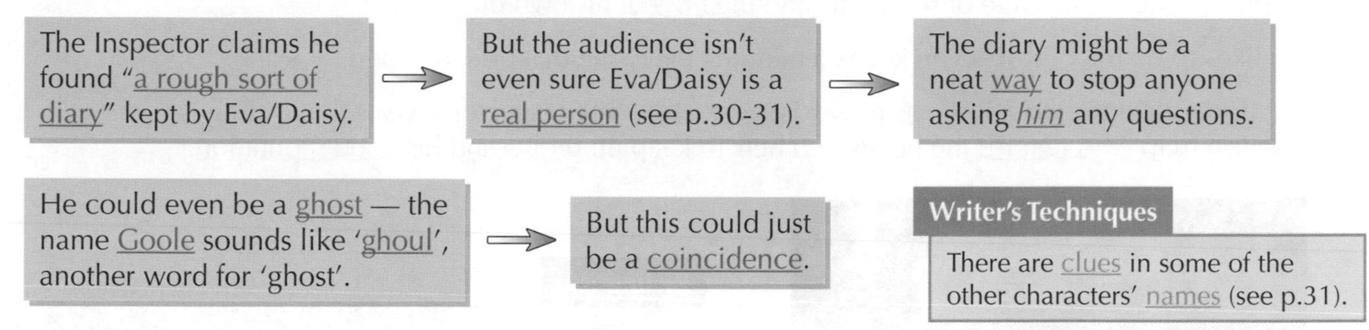

3) Some people think he's meant to be the voice of God or the audience's conscience.

His lesson is more important than who he is

1) When it's revealed that he's not a real police officer, Mr and Mrs Birling don't think he has the authority to judge them and tell them how to behave.
2) Eric and Sheila realise that whether something is morally 'right' or 'wrong' is just as important as whether something is legal or not.

Inspector Goole is mysterious.

The Inspector says what Priestley thinks

A photo of J.B. Priestley.

1) The Inspector is an outsider, but he takes Eva/Daisy's side. He isn't afraid to tell the Birlings what he thinks of them.
2) Priestley uses the Inspector to present his own views. You could say that the Inspector is Priestley's voice in the play.
3) This is most clear in the Inspector's final speech. He's speaking to the Birling family, but it could also be Priestley speaking to the play's audience.
4) Priestley wanted the play to have a strong message about looking after one another, and it's the Inspector's job to deliver it.

See p.37-38 for more on Priestley's views.

I don't have class prejudice — I hate maths *and* geography...

The important thing to remember about the Inspector is that he doesn't seem to belong in 1912 society. With his huge power and knowledge, it almost seems like he could have written the play himself... Hmmm.

Character Profile — Arthur Birling

Arthur Birling's in charge of the Birling family. He's the boss of his own company. He even plays golf with powerful people. He's so obsessed with power that he can't think about anything — or anybody — else.

Arthur Birling is **pretty pleased** with **himself**

1) Arthur Birling is in charge of his family and the boss of his own business.
2) He likes to be in control, so he keeps reminding everyone that he's in charge.
3) But throughout the play, Birling's power is weakened. The Inspector reveals that Birling is a selfish man who ignores the needs of others to keep up profits and his good reputation.

© Simon Gough Photography

Mr Birling likes to be in control of everything.

Birling is...

Ambitious: "there's a very good chance of a knighthood"

A businessman: "practical man of business"

Selfish: "a man has to make his own way"

Worried: "There'll be a public scandal"

He's a successful and ambitious **businessman**

1) Birling treats his daughter's marriage like a business deal. He hopes that his company can join with the company owned by Gerald's father to get "lower costs and higher prices".
2) Birling thinks he's successful because he's a "practical man of business". He has the same practical attitude to the rest of his life.
3) He's hopeful about the future. He thinks that strikes won't cause any problems and doesn't think there will be a war.

Writer's Techniques

Priestley uses dramatic irony to make Birling's opinions seem foolish (see p.47). This makes the audience think that he might be wrong about other things too, for example that socialism is "nonsense".

He **won't accept responsibility** for Eva Smith

Theme — Social Responsibility

Birling laughs at the idea of social responsibility. He calls people like the Inspector "cranks".

1) Birling doesn't think about other people. He doesn't believe in "community and all that nonsense". He only sees the working class as "cheap labour".
2) Birling didn't just refuse to give his workers better wages — he fired the leaders of the strike.
3) Birling only cares about himself. He'd rather forget about Eva and protect his reputation, than face up to what he's done.

Character Profile — Arthur Birling

Birling likes to be *respected*

1) Birling is well known in Brumley and he likes to tell people that he used to be Lord Mayor.
2) When his reputation is threatened he's terrified, and he says that he'd pay to avoid a scandal.
3) He isn't used to someone else being in charge. The Inspector only says twenty words before Birling shows "*impatience*".
4) Birling's family falls apart, and he can't do anything about it. He blames the Inspector for making a "nasty mess".

Mr Birling wants everyone to listen to him.

Underneath it all, Birling is *nervous*

Theme — Social Class

Birling's a rich businessman, but the Crofts are socially 'better' because they inherited land and money.

1) Birling desperately wants Gerald's family to like him. He wants Gerald's parents to know about his knighthood and tries to win Gerald over by getting his father's favourite port.
2) Birling makes himself seem important by telling people about his friendships with powerful people — e.g. he plays golf with the Chief Constable.
3) The Inspector questions whether Birling's company, reputation and powerful friends are really important. Birling gets upset because he has always believed that these things matter.

Birling tries to use *speech* to *stay* in *control*

Priestley uses stage directions and careful language to create Birling's character:

- The actor playing Birling should have a regional accent — this would make it clear that he was middle class and not upper class. The upper class in 1912 did not have regional accents.
- Birling talks the most in the play and doesn't like being interrupted.
- Birling keeps shouting "Rubbish!" to reject what other people have said. But he finishes his own sentences with "of course", to make him sound like he's always right.

Birling's a bad egg — a hard-boiled, practical man of business...

Birling's only thinking about himself, and he's not going to change. He wants his business to make higher profits, but Priestley uses Birling to show that this profit comes at a high cost — people's lives are ruined.

Character Profile — Sybil Birling

Sybil's proud of her reputation and social position — she'll do anything to protect them. For her, they're more important than her children's happiness. Even when the Inspector questions her, she won't back down.

Sybil Birling is **proud** of her **social position**

1) Sybil is very traditional and is stuck in her ways about social class — she's prejudiced against the working class.
2) She thinks that social position is very important and tries to make her family follow the rules of 'proper' behaviour — for example, she tells Sheila off for using slang.
3) These rules of 'proper' behaviour are more important to her than moral rules — what's 'right' and what's 'wrong'.
4) To protect her own status, she's prepared to be cruel. She refuses to let her charity give Eva/Daisy any help.

A prejudice is a negative opinion about someone based on things like class or age.

Sybil is...

Traditional: "There's no need to be disgusting"

Proud: "I was the only one of you who didn't give in to him"

Prejudiced: "a girl of that sort"

Cruel: "I accept no blame"

Sybil is Mr Birling's "**social superior**"

Sybil Birling is from a family with a higher social status than Arthur Birling's family. Even though Arthur is in charge of the family, Sybil is his "*social superior*":

- Sybil tells her husband off for saying the food was good in front of a guest — "Tell cook from me". It wasn't polite to mention servants.
- Sybil won't let anyone boss her around. She tells the Inspector he has "no power" over her.

Mrs Birling thinks that the Inspector is below her.

Sybil lives by **strict standards**

1) Sybil's beliefs about social standards make her prejudiced against the working class.
2) She thinks that they have lower standards.

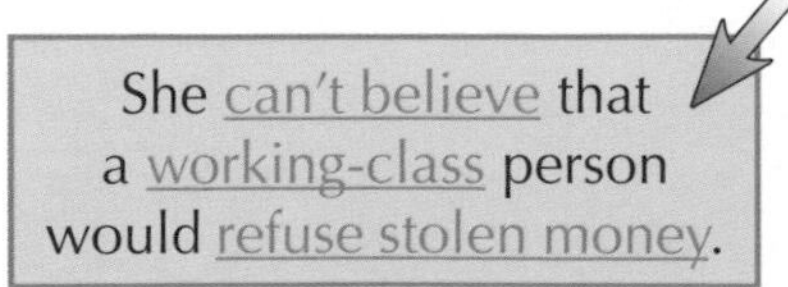
She can't believe that a working-class person would refuse stolen money.

She can't imagine her son being involved with women "of that sort".

3) It's her 'standards' that make her blame the father of Eva/Daisy's unborn child for her suicide, instead of accepting her own guilt.

She thinks that the father is to blame because he shouldn't have got involved with a working-class girl. → She demands that the father should be punished publicly. But she doesn't realise she is actually blaming her own son.

Character Profile — Sybil Birling

Mrs Birling **supports charity** — but she's not very **charitable**

1) Mrs Birling is involved with the Brumley Women's Charity Organisation which she says only supports "deserving cases".
2) She uses her "influence" (social position) to convince the other charity members not to help Eva/Daisy's appeal because she's annoyed about the young woman using the Birling name.
3) She's angry that Eva/Daisy 'pretends' to have the "fine feelings" of a higher social class when she says she turned down stolen money.
4) But Mrs Birling doesn't use her own "fine feelings" to decide whether she should help Eva/Daisy. Instead, she turns her down because of pettiness and class prejudice.

Theme — Social Responsibility

The word "deserving" usually meant poor people who were unable to help themselves. Mrs Birling uses it to mean people who *she thinks* deserve help.

Mrs Birling **doesn't change**

Mrs Birling only cares about herself.

Mrs Birling is self-centred:

- She hasn't noticed her own son's drinking problem.
- She isn't worried that Gerald lost interest in her daughter last summer.
- She won't accept responsibility for Eva/Daisy's suicide, and claims that she was in the 'right' — "I accept no blame".
- She doesn't learn anything from the Inspector.

Stage directions show Mrs Birling has **made** her **mind up**

Even when she speaks politely, her tone is harsh and arrogant:

- The stage directions say that Mrs Birling answers "*sharply*" and "*bitterly*".
- In Act Three, Mrs Birling keeps telling everyone "*triumphantly*" (victoriously) that she knew that the Inspector was a trick. It's more important to her that she comes out on top, than that she could have caused a suicide.
- In the final moments of the play, Mrs Birling is "*smiling*" and tells everyone to feel "amused". This suggests she has already put it all behind her.

Sybil — star of It's-not-my-Faulty Towers

Sybil's so wrapped up in social class and behaving 'properly' that she can't see how she's affected the lives of others. Even her own children. And at the end of the play, she carries on as if nothing happened.

Character Profile — Sheila Birling

At the beginning of the play Sheila seems childish and immature, but as the play goes on she seems more thoughtful, sensitive and sharp. By the end, Sheila wants to start again...

*Sheila seems to be **different** from the rest of her family*

1) Sheila can be as selfish as the rest of her family. A year before the play begins, she used her social position to get Eva/Daisy sacked from her job in a shop.
2) But, she is also clever and strong-minded — she hands Gerald's ring back when she finds out he's had an affair and is wise enough to suspect that Eric is the father of Eva/Daisy's child.
3) By the end of the play, Sheila is sensitive, moral and seems to have changed for good.

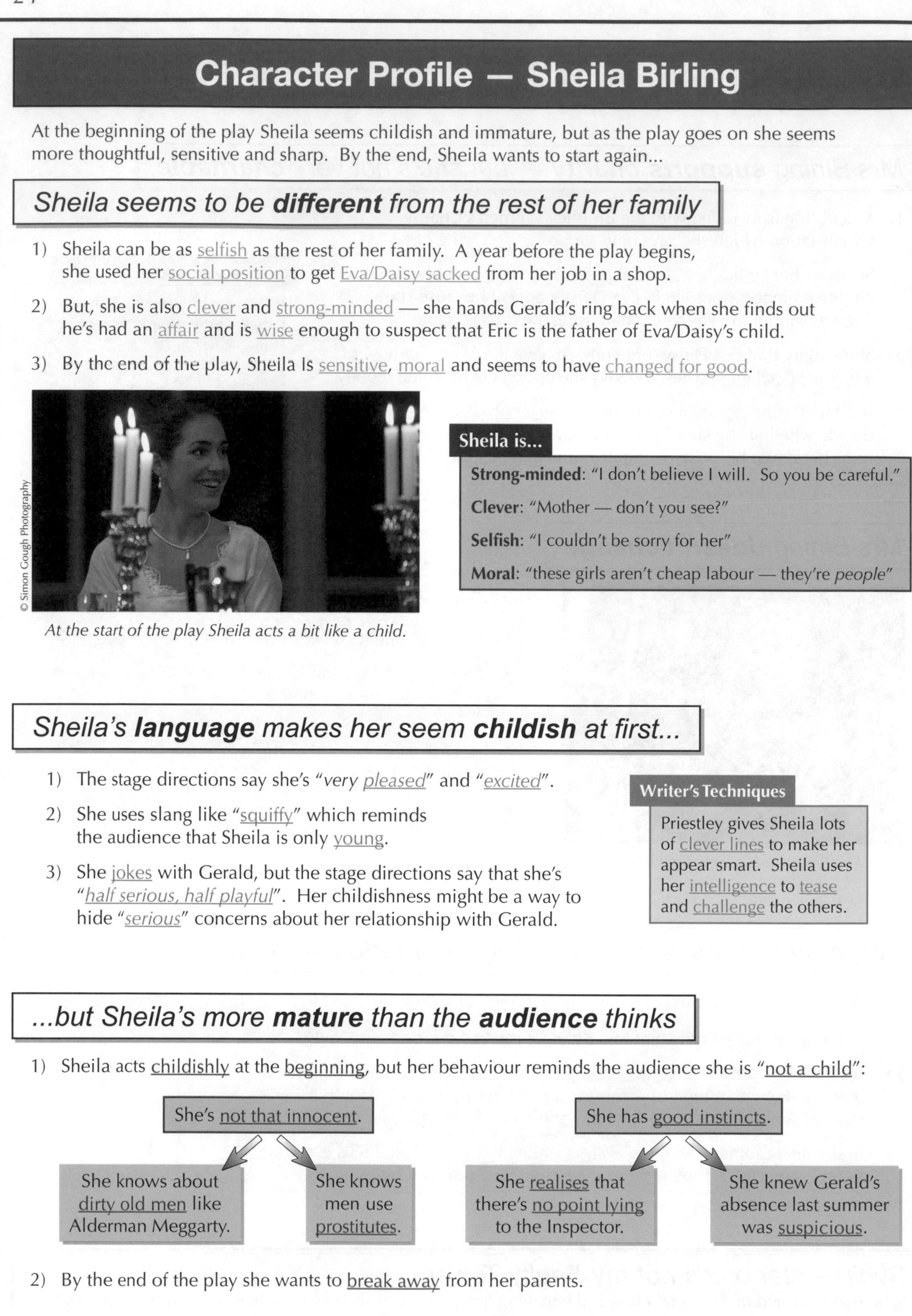

At the start of the play Sheila acts a bit like a child.

Sheila is...

Strong-minded: "I don't believe I will. So you be careful."

Clever: "Mother — don't you see?"

Selfish: "I couldn't be sorry for her"

Moral: "these girls aren't cheap labour — they're *people*"

*Sheila's **language** makes her seem **childish** at first...*

1) The stage directions say she's "*very pleased*" and "*excited*".
2) She uses slang like "squiffy" which reminds the audience that Sheila is only young.
3) She jokes with Gerald, but the stage directions say that she's "*half serious, half playful*". Her childishness might be a way to hide "*serious*" concerns about her relationship with Gerald.

Writer's Techniques

Priestley gives Sheila lots of clever lines to make her appear smart. Sheila uses her intelligence to tease and challenge the others.

*...but Sheila's more **mature** than the **audience** thinks*

1) Sheila acts childishly at the beginning, but her behaviour reminds the audience she is "not a child":

- She's not that innocent.
  - She knows about dirty old men like Alderman Meggarty.
  - She knows men use prostitutes.
- She has good instincts.
  - She realises that there's no point lying to the Inspector.
  - She knew Gerald's absence last summer was suspicious.

2) By the end of the play she wants to break away from her parents.

Character Profile — Sheila Birling

Sheila has **morals**

1) Sheila admits she used her "power" to "punish" Eva/Daisy. She regrets what she did and wants to learn from her mistakes.
2) She acts like a judge at the end of the play — she says "between us we killed her". The other characters never admit that much.
3) She tells Gerald she respects him for being "honest". She also knows the family must stop these "silly pretences". Priestley uses Sheila to show there's hope that people can change.
4) She's the only character who shows real compassion for the working class. She says, "these girls aren't cheap labour — they're *people*."

Theme — Learning about Life

Priestley makes Sheila seem childish at first. This means her treatment of Eva/Daisy could be because she's immature. This makes it easier to forgive her.

The Inspector's **story** changes her for **good**

© Donald Cooper/Rex Features

By the end of the play, Sheila is determined to change.

1) Before Gerald leaves, she gives back the engagement ring, saying that they aren't "the same people who sat down to dinner" — they've changed.
2) After the Inspector goes, her parents want everything to go back to how it was before. Sheila and Eric are the only ones who see that they all have to change.
3) Out of all the characters in the play Sheila changes the most.

Sheila acts a bit like the **Inspector**

1) Sheila wants to know the truth. She takes the Inspector's side and seems to help his investigation. She uses some of his techniques:
   - She asks Gerald as many questions as the Inspector does.
   - She uses shock tactics like revealing Eric's drinking problem to her mother.
   - She challenges and argues with her parents, like the Inspector does. When she's giving the ring back to Gerald she tells her father, "Don't interfere".
2) Sheila realises that the Inspector's questions are meant to break down the "wall" they've put between themselves and Eva/Daisy — Sheila wants to do the same.

Sheila's good at marking — she knows what's right and what's wrong...

Sheila's character offers hope to the audience — she's grown up and realised that she needs to think about what really matters. She lets the Inspector's tragic story affect and change her. Three cheers for Sheila...

Character Profile — Eric Birling

Eric has some issues. He's turned away from his family and taken up drinking. But no one seems to notice, or at least they think it's more polite to not mention it. So, instead, Eric is friendless and alone.

*Eric Birling is a **troubled son***

1) Eric feels like he doesn't belong in his family. He says that no one understands him and he doesn't feel as if he can talk to any of them.
2) Eric apparently forced himself on Eva/Daisy while he was drunk and got her pregnant. He was so drunk he didn't even remember it happening.
3) Eric regrets what he did — by the end of the play he says he'll never forget what he has learnt.

Eric doesn't think he fits in with the family.

Eric is...

Reckless: "I didn't even remember"

Unloved: "You don't understand anything"

Sensitive: "My God — I'm not likely to forget"

A drunk: "he does drink pretty hard"

Priestley** drops hints that Eric **isn't all right

1) Priestley's stage directions say that Eric is "*not quite at ease*". He's described as being "*half shy*".
2) When Gerald jokes that the Inspector might be calling because "Eric's been up to something", Eric acts suspiciously and says that he doesn't think the joke is "very funny".
3) This suggests that he's feeling guilty about something, even though we don't know what he's done until much later.

Writer's Techniques

Priestley uses Eric's strange behaviour to hint that he's hiding secrets that will damage the Birling family's reputation.

*Eric's **hiding** some **dirty secrets***

Eric's drunkenness and bad behaviour represent the dark side of family life.

- He's a heavy drinker, and has been for a while. This is obvious in the way he pours his whisky in Act Three. The rest of the family sees it too.
- He got Eva/Daisy pregnant, and it's suggested that he forced himself on her.
- He has stolen money from his father's business to support her.

If these secrets became public then Birling's knighthood, Sheila's marriage and the whole family's reputation could be ruined.

Character Profile — Eric Birling

*Eric's **not** the only one...*

1) Eric meets Eva/Daisy at the stalls bar when he was looking for women — this is the same place Gerald met her.
2) Birling's "respectable friends" go to the bar to find women. Alderman Meggarty is known to assault young women. They're all behaving badly but no one says anything.
3) These "respectable" men lead pretty unpleasant lives. The play suggests Eric's behaviour is normal for a middle-class man.

*... but he's much more **reckless***

Theme — Learning about Life

His parents don't want a scandal. They don't care about Eric as much as they care about what other people will think.

1) Gerald's affair with Eva/Daisy was less shameful than Eric's because he was more careful. He ended it before his reputation was damaged.
2) The Birlings are shocked by Eric's behaviour because he was reckless — he could have caused a scandal:

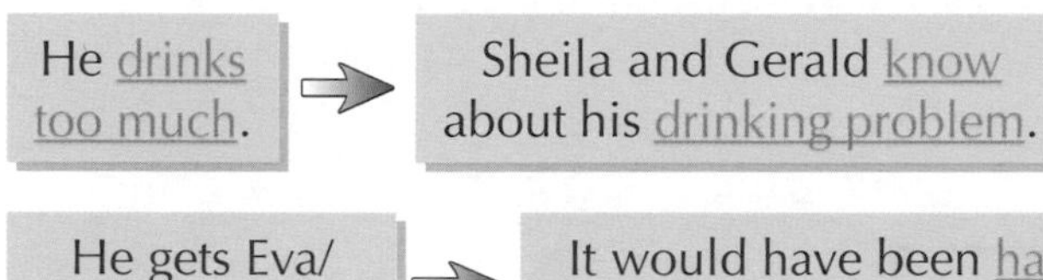

He drinks too much. → Sheila and Gerald know about his drinking problem. → He doesn't keep his drinking secret, so his other secret behaviour could've been found out.

He gets Eva/Daisy pregnant. → It would have been hard for him to ignore Eva/Daisy if she had his child. → If news of a baby got out, it would've ruined the Birling family's reputation.

*Eric is a **villain** and a **victim***

1) Eric feels like he doesn't fit in and that nobody supports him — he's had to find comfort in women and drink.
2) When he shouts at his mother, "You don't understand anything", he's really yelling. It might be the angriest moment in the play.
3) He's obviously a villain in the play, but he accepts responsibility for what he did — "I did what I did". He criticises his parents for pretending nothing's happened.

Theme — Family Life

Birling seems disappointed in his son, and gets on better with Gerald. This must make Eric feel awful.

© Simon Gough Photography

Eric feels terrible for what he did to Eva/Daisy.

Too frisky and two whiskies makes our Eric far too risky...

At first, it might seems like Eric has the worst morals of all the characters. But then he regrets his mistakes and learns from them. The audience start to feel a bit more sorry for him by the end of the play.

Character Profile — Gerald Croft

Gerald's the son-in-law Mr Birling always dreamt of. He's the son of a successful businessman, his mother's a Lady and he seems respectable. Apart from the secret mistress, he's spot on...

Gerald Croft is a **suitable husband**

1) Gerald seems like a good catch. He gets on well with Mr Birling and impresses Sybil Birling.
2) But he's also a liar — he had an affair with Daisy Renton last summer, but told Sheila he was just busy with work.
3) When Gerald finds out that Inspector Goole wasn't a police officer and there was no suicide, he sides with Mr Birling. He wants to protect their reputation.

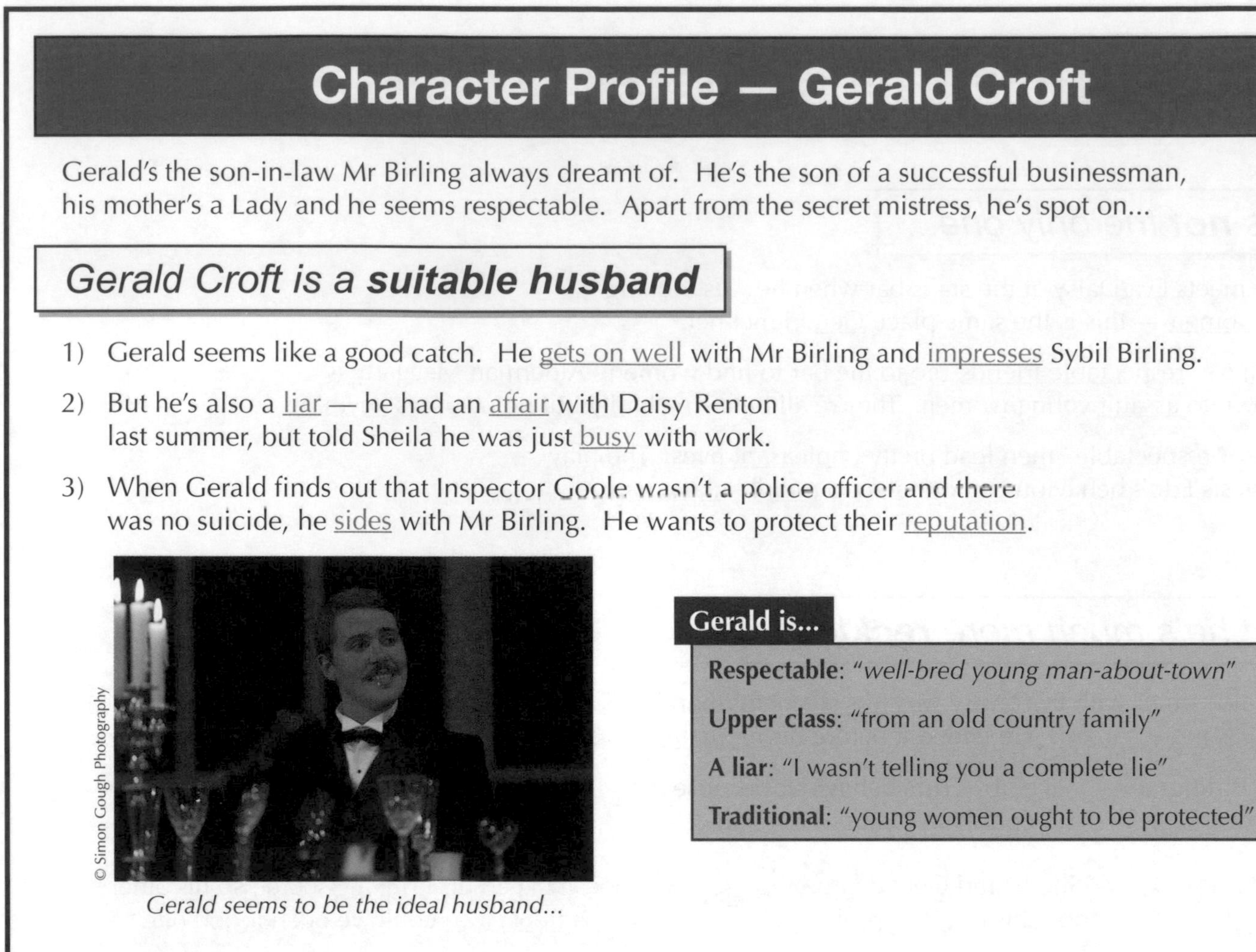

Gerald seems to be the ideal husband...

Gerald is...

Respectable: *"well-bred young man-about-town"*

Upper class: "from an old country family"

A liar: "I wasn't telling you a complete lie"

Traditional: "young women ought to be protected"

Gerald's got a **good future** ahead of him...

1) Gerald's got a lot going for him. He's handsome, wealthy, about thirty — a respectable man-about-town.
2) Unlike the Birlings, he's from a family that inherited money. That makes him their social superior.
3) Gerald works for his father's business 'Crofts Limited'. It's older and bigger than 'Birling and Company', and the two companies are "friendly rivals". He'll probably take over when his father retires.

... but it's a **future** that looks a lot like **Birling's**

Gerald's like a younger version of Arthur Birling.
He's used to, and enjoys, being in control:

- Gerald agrees with Birling about politics and women and laughs at his jokes.
- Like Arthur Birling, he's completely business-minded — he supports Arthur's sacking of Eva Smith: "You couldn't have done anything else."
- They're both more interested in finding out whether the Inspector and the girl were real than learning from what they've done.

Theme — Young and Old

Gerald shows that the younger people in the play can be just as self-centred as the older people. Otherwise you could say that Mr and Mrs Birling don't change because they're too old.

Character Profile — Gerald Croft

Gerald doesn't feel **sorry** for his actions

Gerald doesn't want to learn anything from the Inspector's visit:

- He's the first character to use the word "hoax" (trick) — he's keen to prove the Inspector was a fake and clear everyone's names.
- At the end of the play, he says "Everything's all right now, Sheila". He doesn't seem to have learnt anything.

© Donald Cooper

Gerald wants to pretend nothing's happened.

He thinks he's done **nothing wrong** — but he's just as much to **blame**

Theme — Social Class

Gerald made Eva/Daisy happy, but he still treated her badly because she was working class. He only looked after her while it suited him.

1) Gerald says that Eva/Daisy "didn't blame me". The audience might not blame Gerald at first because Eva/Daisy didn't.
2) The Inspector isn't too harsh on him because Gerald had "affection" for Daisy and made her "happy".
3) But then he left her and went away. He basically made her homeless.

Gerald's not simply **bad** or **good**

You can't say that Gerald is all good or all bad — he's a complicated character.

A hypocrite is someone who says one thing but then does the opposite.

1) Gerald is confident but he's also stubborn — he doesn't learn much in the play. The Inspector points out that Gerald is a hypocrite:
   - The Inspector asks Gerald whether he thinks young women should be "protected" from "unpleasant" things. Gerald says yes, thinking of Sheila.
   - But it's people like Gerald who are doing the unpleasant things to women like Eva/Daisy — he uses her and then gets rid of her. He's no different to Mr Birling and other men who have the same attitudes.
2) Gerald is able to protect his public, respectable image from his private life — something Eric struggles to do. Eric's drinking problem is widely known, and Eva/Daisy could have told Mrs Birling's charity that Eric was the father of her child if she'd wanted to.

Gerald's not shallow — he's just emotionally challenged...

Gerald's upset when he learns that Daisy's dead, but he gets over it pretty quickly. He refuses to let a fake inspector play a prank on him — he'd rather keep up his reputation and win Sheila back.

Character Profile — Eva Smith / Daisy Renton

Who was Eva Smith? Were Eva Smith and Daisy Renton the same person? Was she even real? We never find out the answers to these questions. What matters most is what Eva/Daisy represents.

*Who was **Eva Smith**?*

1) Eva Smith worked for Arthur Birling until she was sacked for protesting against low wages. This set off the chain of events that eventually led to her death — and all the Birlings were involved.
2) According to the Inspector, Eva Smith changed her name to Daisy Renton.

It isn't clear who Eva/Daisy really was.

3) The real identity of Eva/Daisy is never revealed. She could be the same person or different people. The Birlings see and treat all working-class girls the same way, so it doesn't matter who she really was.

Eva/Daisy is...

Attractive: "young and fresh"

Honourable: "she didn't want to take stolen money"

Working class: "a girl of that sort"

*The Birlings **take away** all of Eva/Daisy's **earnings***

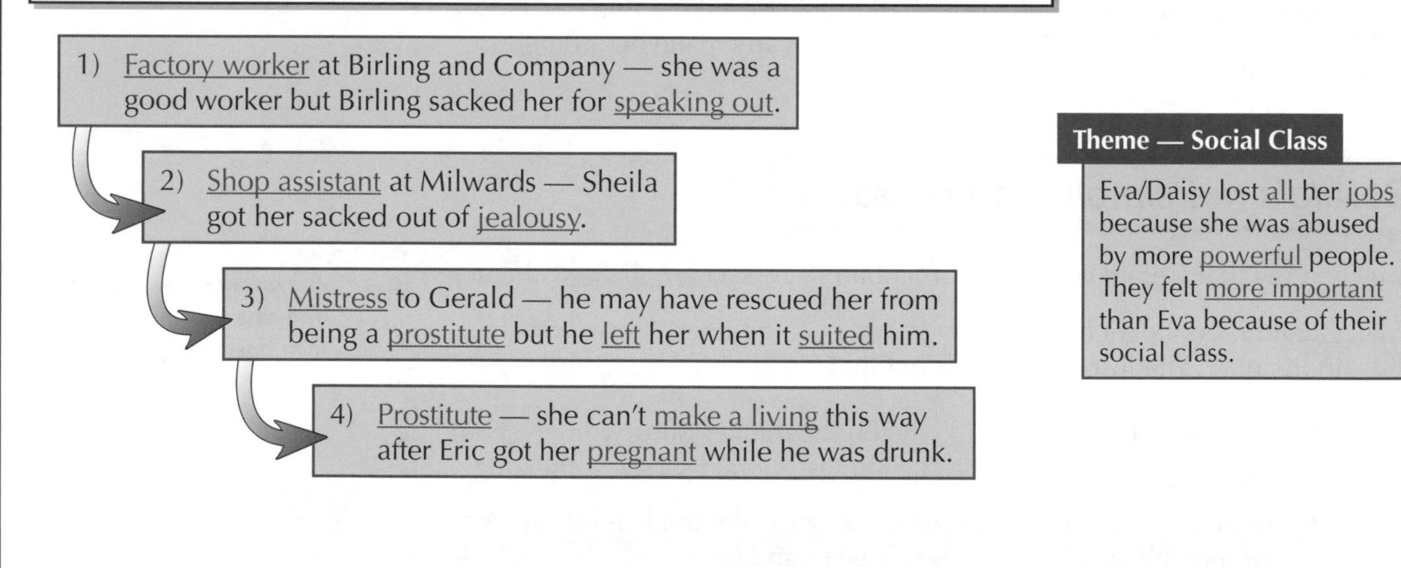

Theme — Social Class

Eva/Daisy lost all her jobs because she was abused by more powerful people. They felt more important than Eva because of their social class.

*She **never** tried to get **revenge** — the **Inspector** does it for her*

1) Eva/Daisy is a silent character who represents the powerless members of society.
2) Maybe Eva/Daisy didn't feel that she was able to make life difficult for the people who mistreated her.
3) Inspector Goole speaks for Eva/Daisy and uses her to teach the Birlings about social responsibility.

Character Profile — Eva Smith / Daisy Renton

*Were **Eva Smith** and **Daisy Renton** the **same person**?*

1) Gerald thinks there were lots of different girls. He says that there was more than one photograph and they have "no proof it was the same girl."
2) But Gerald also says that Daisy Renton told him she had to leave a "job in one of the works" and "about the shop too" — so Eva Smith must be Daisy Renton. But...

- The phone call at the end of the play confuses everything. Has Eva/Daisy just committed suicide? Was the Inspector a ghost, or was he from the future?
- Or is this a phone call about a different girl? The Inspector warned that everyone's lives are "intertwined" (directly linked) — the Birlings don't know how many lives they have affected.

The last phone call leaves a lot of unanswered questions.

*Eva represents **all working-class women***

Eva Smith is supposed to be an ordinary working-class girl. Priestley leaves clues in her name:

This sounds like Eve, the first woman in the Bible — she could represent all women.

+

SMITH

This is a very common last name. It also comes from the word for someone who works with their hands e.g. a blacksmith, locksmith.

=

EVA SMITH

Her name could mean that she represents all ordinary, working-class women.

*Eva Smith is **key** to the play's **message***

1) The Inspector says that there are "millions of Eva Smiths and John Smiths" and that everybody's happiness is connected.
2) This is the key point — the Inspector is telling the Birlings, and the audience, to behave responsibly towards others.
3) Even though we never see her, the focus of the play is the life and death of an unknown woman. Even if they all met different girls, it doesn't matter. Eva/Daisy is a mix of all the people they've ever treated badly.

Theme — Social Responsibility

Eva/Daisy represents all the vulnerable working-class people who need the support of a more caring society.

Gerald ♥ Daisy 4 Eva — or for the summer of 1911 at least...

It's pretty weird to think that every single thing you do can affect someone else. It's true though. Priestley uses Eva/Daisy as a way of showing his audience how everyone is responsible for one another.

Practice Questions

Congratulations — that's another section done. As a special reward for your hard work, here's a trophy and a huge cake. Oh no, sorry, it's two pages of practice questions. Well, don't spend too long on these quick questions — just use them to warm up for the next page. Happy days.

Quick Questions

Q1 How does the Inspector treat the Birlings?

Q2 Summarise the message of the Inspector's speech in one sentence.

Q3 Give two examples of how Birling tries to stay in control.

Q4 Give one example of what Mrs Birling thinks about the working class.

Q5 In one sentence, describe how Sheila comes across at the beginning of the play.

Q6 Name two ways in which Sybil and Sheila are different from each other.

Q7 Find a quote to show that Eric regrets his actions.

Q8 Who or what does the character of Eva Smith represent?

Practice Questions

Now for the biggies. You should be practiced, warmed-up and raring to go. Write a few lines for the in-depth questions, and then write a full-length answer for the exam-style questions. Imagine you're sitting in the exam hall, chewing the end of your pen, and you've got a side or two of paper to fill for each question.

In-depth Questions

Q1 Who or what do you think the Inspector is? Do you think that Priestley wants us to know?

Q2 How and why does Priestley use dramatic irony to show that Mr Birling is foolish?

Q3 Do you think Mrs Birling learns anything about social responsibility from the Inspector? Use quotations from the text to back up your answer.

Q4 Is Gerald more similar to Mr and Mrs Birling or Eric and Sheila? Explain your answer.

Exam-style Questions

Q1 Explain how Priestley presents Eric in *An Inspector Calls*.

Think about:
- What Eric says and does
- How Eric treats the other characters in the play

Q2 Look again at the passage in Act Two from "Inspector: Why didn't she want to take any more money from him?" to "Mrs Birling: Certainly. I consider it your duty. And now no doubt you'd like to say good night."

What do you think about the way that Mrs Birling acts in this passage?

Write about:
- Her attitudes towards the working class
- How she talks to the Inspector

Britain in 1912 and 1945

An Inspector Calls is set in 1912, but it was written for audiences in 1945. That means you've got to think about how audiences in 1945 would have reacted to the issues in the play.

Men and women were treated differently in 1912

Women in 1912 didn't have the same freedom as they did in 1945.

1912

1) Men and women weren't equal — women weren't allowed to vote.
2) Upper and middle-class women like Sheila relied on their husbands and fathers to protect and provide for them.

1945

1) By 1945, all men and women over 21 could vote. This meant women had more power.
2) During the Second World War, women from all classes got jobs to help the war effort. This meant that after the war women had more independence — they'd proved they could work as hard as men.

By 1945 the class system was a bit fairer

In 1912, the working classes had to work hard for low wages. By 1945, things were starting to get better.

1912

1) British society was divided into classes. The people with the most money had the most power.
2) The three main classes were the upper class (e.g. Gerald's family) who had the most power, followed by the middle class (e.g. the Birlings) who had some power, and then the working class (e.g. Eva/Daisy) who were mostly powerless.
3) If a working-class family fell on hard times, there wasn't much help available. That's why charities like Sybil's were very important.

Working-class miners protesting low wages in 1912.

1945

1) Britain was still divided into classes, but things were getting fairer.
2) Millions of people from all classes fought for Britain in the Second World War. After the war, people wanted a fairer society and ideas like socialism became popular. Audiences in 1945 would have been more open to the idea of social responsibility.
3) The Labour Party won the 1945 General Election by lots of votes. Labour focused on looking after the poorest people in society. This shows how attitudes towards helping the working class were beginning to change.

Key Quote

Birling: "it's my duty to keep labour costs down".

Socialism is the idea that money and power should be shared more equally.

The play's still popular today — perhaps it's just as important...

An Inspector Calls looks at society in 1912 — but the play still can get us to think about today's problems: money, sexism and whether society is fair. What a barrel of laughs this play is...

Family Life

At the start, Gerald thinks that the Birlings are "a nice well-behaved family". But the play shows that not everything is as it seems. There are nasty secrets hidden behind the Birlings' polite behaviour.

Families in *1912* were supposed to *behave correctly*

1) Family members were supposed to know their place — the parents were in charge of the family, and the children were expected to do as they were told.
2) In middle-class families, men and women were supposed to behave in a certain way:

Key Quote

Gerald: "You seem to be a nice well-behaved family".

Men were expected to...

- Work to support their family.
- Protect women — especially their wives and daughters.

Women were expected to...

- Marry someone with money so they didn't have to work.
- Plan parties, visit friends and have children. They had staff to do jobs like washing, cooking or cleaning.

The *Birlings* seem *normal* but something's *not right*

1) The Birlings want everyone to believe they're the perfect family.
2) But in Act One, there's tension hiding just under the surface:

- Mrs Birling keeps correcting her family's social mistakes, e.g. she tells Sheila off for using slang.
- Eric laughs randomly and acts strangely.
- When Sheila teases Gerald, she's half playful, but *"half serious"*, about him ignoring her last summer.

Photo: An Inspector Calls, ©2010 Lamb's Players Theatre

The Birlings seem like a nice, normal family.

3) The Inspector's visit encourages Sheila and Eric to stand up for themselves:

- Sheila doesn't know whether she'll marry Gerald any more. She needs time to decide for herself.
- Eric confronts his mother and tells her she doesn't "understand anything".
- Eric tells his parents that he's "ashamed" of them.

4) Sheila and Eric refuse to pretend any more. They won't do what their parents tell them to do.

And I thought my family had problems...

Once the truth comes out, the Birlings aren't playing happy families any more. It's more a case of: Mr Birling the bully, Master Birling the boozer and Mr Croft the creep. It's nothing like that card game I used to play...

Social Class

Social class is really important in *An Inspector Calls*. Class affects how the Birlings behave, and how they treat people. The class system had been around for a long time and Priestley didn't agree with it.

*The **plot** and the **characters** focus on **class***

Photo: An Inspector Calls, ©20˙0 Lamb's Players Theatre

The Inspector challenges the class system.

1) The characters in the play represent the different classes. Priestley wants the audience to see how unfairly the working class was treated by the upper classes.
2) Class is really important to the plot because Priestley's message is about social responsibility.
3) Priestley wants people to look out for each other no matter what class they are. Everybody is connected and shouldn't be separated by class prejudice.

Key Quote

Mrs Birling: "She (Eva) was giving herself ridiculous airs."

*There was a clear **class structure** in the **early 20th century***

The class you belonged to mostly depended on how much money you had. There were three main classes:

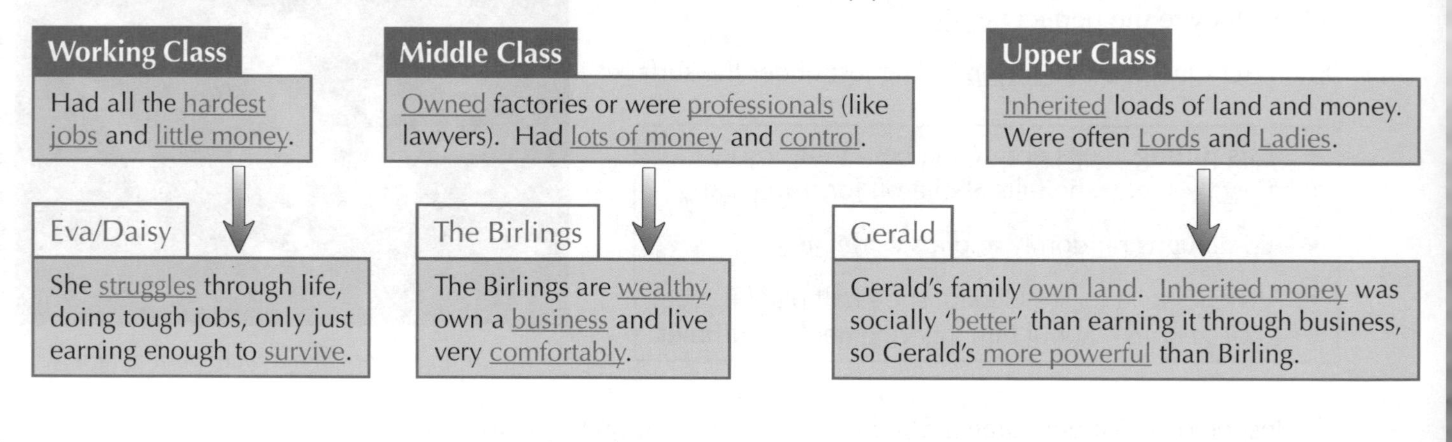

*The **class system** meant the **working class struggled***

1) The class system made life difficult for the working class — it was hard for people like Eva/Daisy to help themselves if they were in trouble.
2) The upper classes in the play don't feel responsible for the working class. They either:

OR DIDN'T WANT TO KNOW OR DIDN'T CARE

3) Priestley suggests that the richest members of society didn't want to change the class system because they didn't want to share their money or power.

Social Class

*The **Birlings** think **class** is all that **matters***

1) Birling's biggest worry about Eva/Daisy's death is that he won't get his knighthood because there will be a "scandal".
2) Birling thinks he's important because he was Lord Mayor and has had other powerful positions.
3) Birling uses Gerald to raise his social class. Birling wants Gerald's parents to know that he's expecting a knighthood. He's also happy that Sheila's marriage to Gerald will move her into a higher class.
4) Mrs Birling is involved in a charity but it seems like she's only doing it for the social status.

Priestley** thought **class shouldn't matter

1) The play isn't just about one family's scandal. It was how Priestley saw society.
2) The Birlings' arrogance and selfish attitudes were meant to be common in the middle classes. His characters represent the worst qualities of the upper and middle classes.
3) Priestley shows how unfair the class system was for working-class people like Eva/Daisy. Although we only hear Eva/Daisy's story, the problems she faced were probably quite common. Eva Smith could have been anyone.

What class you were in even mattered to children.

*How people **act** isn't just about **class***

1) Eva/Daisy is expected to have no morals because she's from the working class, but she refuses to accept stolen money even when she's desperate.
2) The Birlings think that class is all that matters, but Priestley believed the opposite. He wants people to be judged by what they do, not by which class they belong to.
3) At the end of the play, Sheila and Eric realise they have a responsibility to the working class. Priestley shows that people can choose to act differently from the rest of their class.

Writer's Techniques

Eva/Daisy is presented as more honourable than the middle and upper classes. This might have surprised some of Priestley's audience.

Mrs Birling might be from the upper class but she's not very classy...

The Inspector doesn't seem to fit into the class structure. Instead, he pulls it apart. He challenges the attitudes of Sheila and Eric and makes them want to change — this makes the audience question their own beliefs.

Social Responsibility

The play's purpose is to show how important social responsibility is. Social responsibility is the idea that everyone should be responsible for each other because our actions affect everybody else.

The *characters'* views are *challenged*

The Inspector shows how each of the characters were responsible for Eva/Daisy's suicide. Sheila and Eric learn from the Inspector's visit, but Mr and Mrs Birling refuse to change.

Birling...

... thinks that social responsibility is "nonsense". Making a profit is more important than worker's rights.

Mrs Birling...

... believes that she has no responsibility to the working class — her prejudices are so deep that they can't be changed.

Sheila...

... realised that getting Eva/Daisy sacked wasn't very responsible — but she didn't do anything about it at the time. She wants to improve her behaviour.

Eric...

... realises that taking advantage of Eva/Daisy was irresponsible and that he ruined her chances of improving her life.

Social responsibility is the Inspector's main *focus*

1) The Inspector's final speech is clear and to the point — it's a summary of what he's tried to teach the Birlings about responsibility.
2) The Inspector isn't just trying to make the family feel guilty, he wants to make them aware of the problems faced by all of the working class.

Key Quote

Inspector: "We are responsible for each other."

All the events in the play are connected. Priestley's moral seems to be that it doesn't take great people to change the world — we can all change it by the way we treat others.

The *play tells* you a lot about Priestley's *socialist* ideas

1) Priestley supported socialism — his plays encourage social responsibility and criticise the class system.
2) *An Inspector Calls* tries to make the audience question their own social responsibility.
3) Birling is wrong about lots of things, like the "unsinkable" *Titanic* and the start of the war. This means that when Birling says that socialism is "nonsense", the audience thinks he's wrong about that too.

Socialism is the idea that money and power should be shared more equally.

The most important lesson is to 'care about others' — I thought it was ICT...

Not really — I can barely use a computer. As his name suggests, Priestley is a bit preachy, but that's the whole point of the play. He wants to encourage social responsibility as much as he can...

Young and Old

The Inspector, and his story about Eva/Daisy, divides the young and the old in the play. The older generation want to forget the Inspector's visit ever happened — the younger generation want to make them remember...

The **older** and the **younger generations** are very **different**

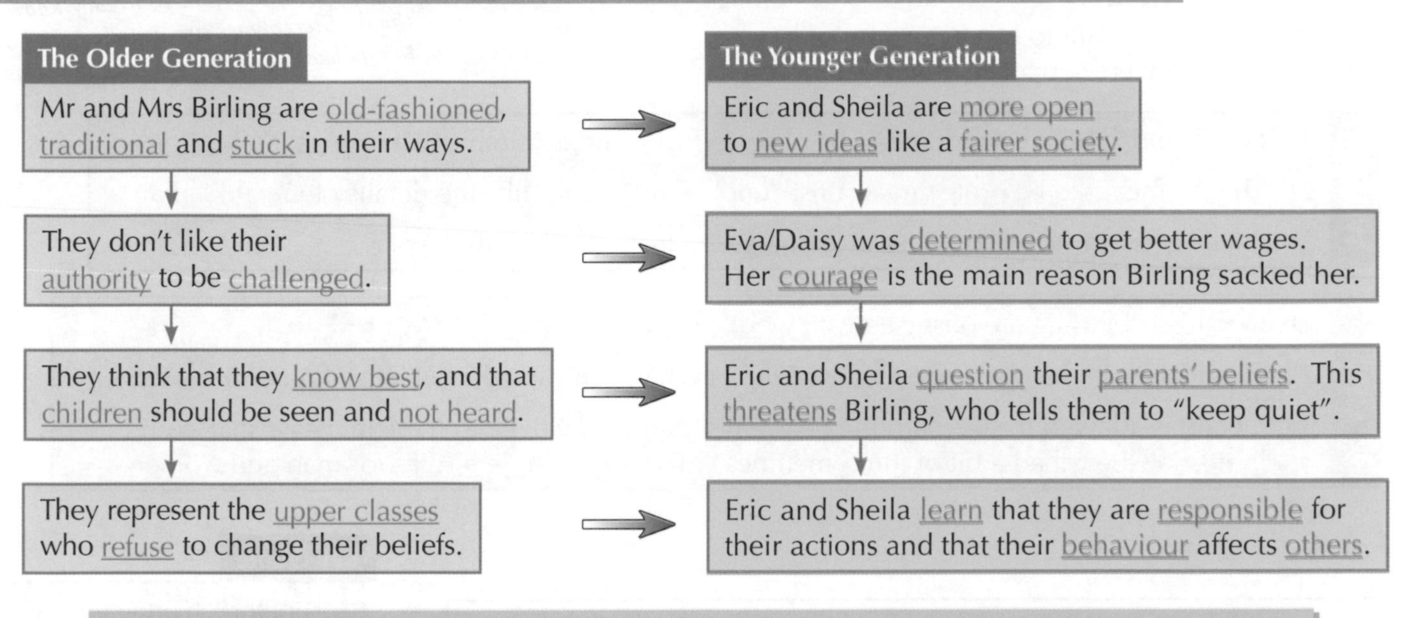

Because Eric and Sheila learn from their mistakes, there's hope for a fairer society in the future.

Gerald's the **oldest** young man around

1) Gerald's closer to Sheila and Eric's age than he is to Mr and Mrs Birling's, but he's a young man who's already old in his attitudes. He's a younger version of Arthur:

   - His marriage to Sheila is for business reasons.
   - He agrees that Eva/Daisy had to be sacked.

2) He doesn't learn anything:

   - When it's revealed that he ditched Daisy/Eva, he doesn't seem to feel that guilty.
   - At the end, he thinks his marriage to Sheila is back on.

3) Gerald is from the younger generation but, unlike Sheila and Eric, he doesn't change. This suggests that a fairer future isn't certain — people can choose whether to change or not.

Key Quote

Mr Birling (sarcastically): "the famous younger generation who know it all."

Gerald doesn't fit in with the younger generation.

With this book you can be the famous younger generation who know it all...

When I was a child they kept telling me that I was the future — now they tell me that you're the future... I wish they'd make up their minds. Priestley thought that the younger generation were the future too.

Men and Women

In 1912, men and women had different roles in the family and society. Priestley wants his audience to think about the way men and women were treated and whether their different roles were fair.

The **men** and **women** start out as **stereotypes**

A stereotype is an idea you might have about people before you really know them. Stereotypes are usually based on things like a person's sex, age and class.

The characters are meant to be stereotypes of how men and women were supposed to act in 1912:

WOMEN

1) Sheila and Sybil are supposed to be obsessed with "pretty clothes", shopping and weddings.
2) They're meant to be protected against "unpleasant" things like the details of Gerald's affair.
3) Sheila gets Eva sacked because of jealousy — a female quality in the play.

MEN

1) Gerald and Birling are obsessed with work and public affairs.
2) Gerald feels it's his duty to rescue Eva/Daisy from the unwanted attentions of Alderman Meggarty.
3) Gerald is allowed to sleep around before his marriage. Sheila isn't. Arthur says that even in his day they "had a bit of fun sometimes". There are different rules for men and women.

Key Quote

Inspector: "young women ought to be protected"

The **young women challenge** the **stereotypes**

Men had more power than women — women were expected to do what they were told by their fathers, husbands or bosses. Eva/Daisy and Sheila refuse to do what society expects of them:

- Eva/Daisy questioned whether her wages were fair instead of accepting them.
- Eva/Daisy refused to rely on Eric, and rejected his stolen money.
- By the end of the play, Sheila interrupts and challenges everyone (apart from the Inspector).

By the **end** the **stereotypes** are turned **upside down**

1) As the play develops, Birling, Gerald and Eric get weaker, while Sheila gets stronger.
2) Gerald is rejected by Sheila, and Eric is revealed to have a drinking problem. Birling suffers the most — the whole night has weakened his control over his family.
3) Sheila starts giving her own opinions, not those she's 'supposed' to have. She's learnt to think for herself.

© Simon Gough Photography

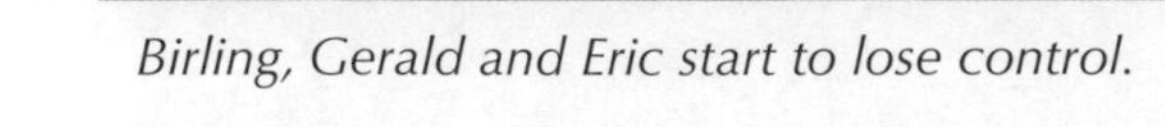

Birling, Gerald and Eric start to lose control.

Priestley's a writer with an a-gender...

The Birlings use stereotypes to help them decide who they like and don't like before even getting to know them. I'd much rather people decided they didn't like me once they'd gotten to know me — but then again...

Learning about Life

This play presents a harsh world where innocent people suffer. You've got to learn fast. Some innocents — like Eva/Daisy's baby — die without ever having a chance.

Some people **never learn...**

1) Birling makes fun of Eric's private education and the younger generation who "know it all", because he made his own fortune. This is ironic because it's mainly the older generation who think they know it all.
2) Birling's arrogance makes him stubborn. He doesn't think anyone can tell him anything useful. He only listens to Gerald because he's from the upper class.
3) Birling, Sybil and Gerald's arrogance prevents them from changing. They don't see anything wrong in the way they think or act. They believe that they know best.

... others **try** to **change**

1) The Inspector has much more of an effect on Eric and Sheila, who feel guilty about their behaviour. They turn their backs on their parents for not learning from what's happened.
2) They realise that the important thing about the evening was the lesson, not whether the Inspector was real.
3) Sheila changes her views and her personality — she starts out playful, selfish and obedient, but by the end she is more aware, sensitive and mature.

© Simon Gough Photography

At the end of the play, Sheila refuses to listen to her parents.

The older generation **don't want** to **know**

Key Quote

Sheila: "you don't seem to have learnt anything."

1) One of the reasons the older generation won't change is that they're happy not knowing about working-class problems. They aren't affected by things like poverty, so they don't want to hear about it.
2) In fact, they don't like to think about anything bad:
   - Prostitution — "I see no point in mentioning the subject," says Birling.
   - Womanising — "you don't mean Alderman Meggarty?" says Mrs Birling, even though it's well-known.
   - Drinking — "It isn't true," says Mrs Birling when Eric's drinking problem is revealed.
3) They do everything they can to avoid changing, even when it's obvious that they've done something wrong — they refuse to believe it, and blame everyone else instead.

I wanted to know how jelly was made — now I wish I didn't know...

If you don't know, don't look it up. It's better that way. Anyway, back to the play... For Sheila and Eric, learning about the world (as it really is) helps them see their own selfish views in a new light.

Practice Questions

These quick questions are designed to get you thinking, so don't worry about writing lots and lots.
Just jot down a few quick words for each one and then pat yourself on the back for a good job well done.

Quick Questions

Q1 Give two examples of things that were different in 1912 compared to 1945.

Q2 Give one example of how middle-class women were supposed to behave in 1912.

Q3 Which class is represented by each of the following characters?
a) Gerald b) Arthur Birling c) Eva Smith

Q4 Why is Birling glad that Sheila is marrying Gerald?

Q5 What is social responsibility?

Q6 Give two ways that Gerald is more like the older generation than the younger.

Q7 What is a stereotype?

Q8 Give one reason why the Birlings refuse to change their ways.

Practice Questions

These theme questions are a bit trickier than the questions about plot and characters — but any of this could come up in the exam, so make sure you're ready by having a go at these in-depth and exam-style questions.

In-depth Questions

Q1 How does Priestley's presentation of the Birlings make you feel about the middle class in 1912?

Q2 Why do you think Priestley made Eva/Daisy more moral than the Birlings?

Q3 Do you think Sheila fits the stereotype for middle-class women in 1912? Explain your answer.

Q4 Explain why the Birlings don't want to know about working-class problems.

Exam-style Questions

Q1 What message is Priestley trying to present about social class in *An Inspector Calls*?

Think about:
- How he presents the characters in the play
- What the Inspector says and does

Q2 Look again at the passage in Act Three from "Eric: (sulkily) I'm all right" to "Eric: (quietly, bitterly) I don't give a damn now whether I stay here or not."

How does Priestley present the conflict between the two generations in this passage?

Think about:
- How Eric and Sheila react to the play's events
- How Mr and Mrs Birling react to the play's events
- The way the different generations speak to each other

'An Inspector Calls' on the Stage

An Inspector Calls is a play — don't call it a book or a novel. Priestley wrote it for the stage — to be seen and heard. These pages are about how the play is performed on the stage.

One set can be used for the **whole play**

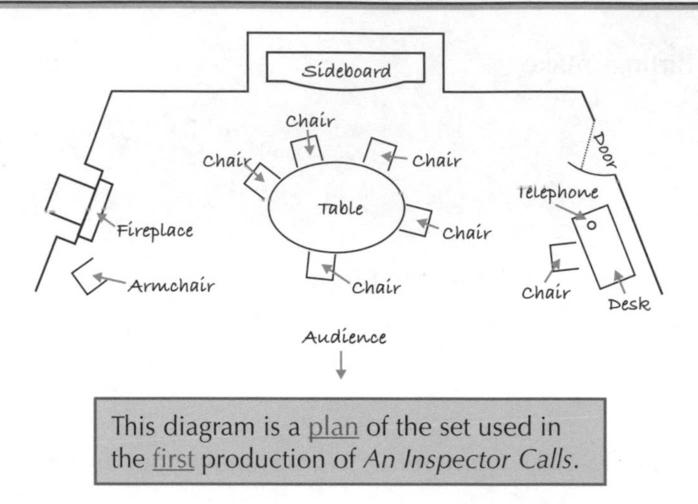

This diagram is a plan of the set used in the first production of *An Inspector Calls*.

1) All the action takes place in the Birlings' dining room — the whole play can be staged using one set.
2) The set is cramped which makes the atmosphere of the play seem intense.
3) The small set shows how self-centred the Birlings are and how unwelcome an outsider (the Inspector) is.

There are **warning signs** from the **beginning**

1) A good production of the play should show how the family falls apart as their secrets are revealed.
2) Even before the Inspector arrives, the audience should see that there are problems:

- The actress playing Sheila should be "*half serious, half playful*" with Gerald. This will show she already has doubts about him.
- The actor playing Eric has to seem half drunk — for example, he toasts Sheila and Gerald "*rather noisily*". This hints at his drinking problem.

The way the play **looks** can say a lot about its **message**

1) The lighting is "*pink*" at the start, as if everything is warm and lovely. But it becomes "*brighter and harder*" when the Inspector arrives — as if a spotlight is turned on their world.
2) The Birlings and Gerald are dressed in smart clothes to show how rich they are. In contrast, Inspector Goole is dressed simply.
3) Stephen Daldry's production put the Birling's house on stilts, high above a street. This suggests that the Birlings look down on other people, and that their world could easily collapse.

Writer's Techniques

Priestley's stage directions say how the play should look. But productions can change the set, lighting and costumes to suit their 'take' on the play.

'An Inspector Calls'? More like 'An Inspector Ruins Everything'...

Look closely at everything — from the lighting instructions to the set design, and even the little stage directions. These details are all part of the play and they're just as important as the dialogue.

Dramatic Techniques in 'An Inspector Calls'

Priestley uses all the tricks in the book to make his play as dramatic and tense as possible.
Well, apart from trick number 38: a dangerous car chase through the streets of Brumley.

Priestley ***builds tension*** *during the play*

Act One & Two

The Inspector increases the tension by only releasing information bit by bit. For example he only shows the photo(s) to one person at a time. This keeps the characters, and the audience, on their toes.

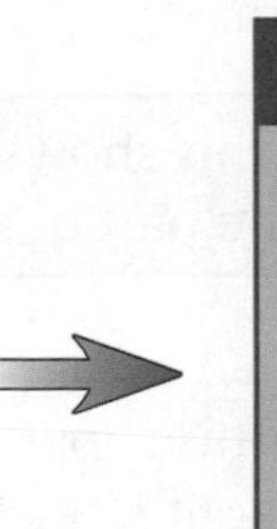

Act Two

At the beginning of Act Two, the audience expects to hear Gerald confess, but the focus shifts to Sheila and Sybil. This builds tension because the audience are left in suspense.

Act Three

In Act One, the family are seated, but by the end the characters are standing, shouting, drinking and crying. The tension has increased to the point where the Birlings are falling apart.

Entrances *and* ***exits*** *are* ***important***

1) The Inspector arrives just as Birling says "a man has to mind his own business". It's as if the Inspector has been sent to prove the exact opposite.
2) When characters exit the stage they're usually escaping someone or something — e.g. Sheila runs off the stage when she realises that getting Eva/Daisy sacked may have led to her suicide.
3) The Inspector uses exits to help get information out of the other characters — e.g. the Inspector leaves Sheila and Gerald alone to discuss his affair with Daisy Renton.

The ***beginnings*** *and* ***ends*** *of the acts are* ***dramatic moments***

Priestley freezes the action between Acts to create tension.

- Act One ends with the Inspector asking "Well?". Act Two opens with the same moment. The audience will wonder about the answer to his question during the break, which adds to the suspense.
- The end of Act Two is another cliffhanger. Eric comes back, but Priestley makes the audience wait until Act Three for Eric's confession.

The Inspector's questions build the tension.

Goole is like Inspector Gadget — Go(ole), Go(ole) Gadget Tension...

If you just look at the plot in terms of action, it seems as if nothing really happens — it's just people in a room. But Priestley's dramatic techniques make the Birlings' stories seem like flashbacks in a film.

The Language of 'An Inspector Calls'

An audience can tell a lot about a character from the words they use and the way they say them.

*The characters' **language** reveals **more** about them*

The words used by the characters tell the audience a lot about them.

Birling family → Use upper-class language like "chaps" (men). → This shows that they want to be part of the upper class.

Sheila and Eric → Use slang e.g. "squiffy". Mrs Birling is shocked and tells them not to. → This shows their youth and the conflict between the young and old.

Mr Birling → Talks in business language — he says they were "sold" (tricked) by the fake Inspector. → This shows he only sees the world in business terms.

Inspector Goole** uses language **differently

1) The Inspector uses plain, direct language and only says what he needs to. This contrasts with Birling's wordy speeches.
2) He makes people feel uneasy by staring at them in silence for a while before he speaks to them.
3) The older Birlings think he's "rude" because of his manner and language.

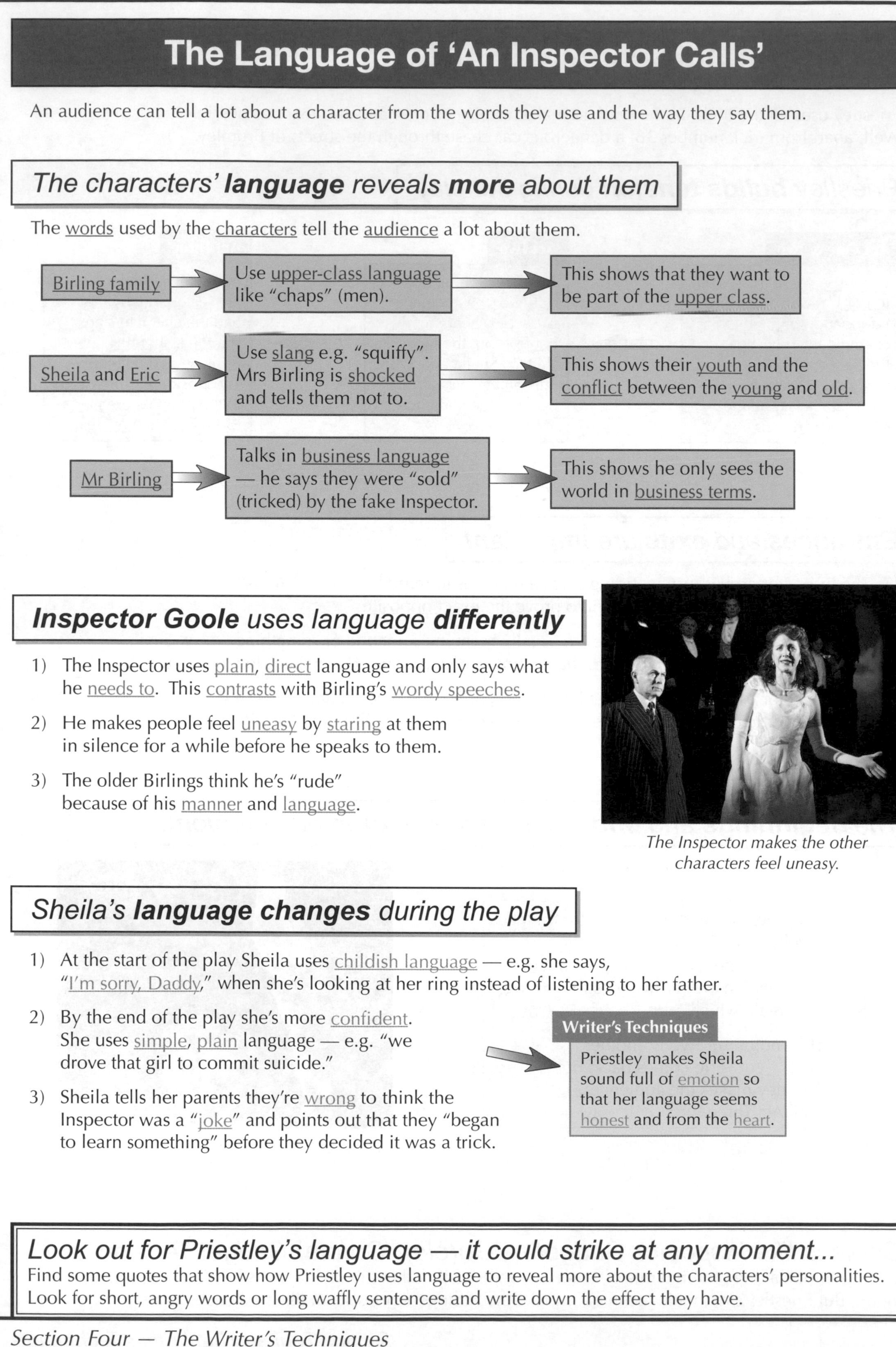

The Inspector makes the other characters feel uneasy.

*Sheila's **language changes** during the play*

1) At the start of the play Sheila uses childish language — e.g. she says, "I'm sorry, Daddy," when she's looking at her ring instead of listening to her father.
2) By the end of the play she's more confident. She uses simple, plain language — e.g. "we drove that girl to commit suicide."
3) Sheila tells her parents they're wrong to think the Inspector was a "joke" and points out that they "began to learn something" before they decided it was a trick.

Writer's Techniques

Priestley makes Sheila sound full of emotion so that her language seems honest and from the heart.

Look out for Priestley's language — it could strike at any moment...

Find some quotes that show how Priestley uses language to reveal more about the characters' personalities. Look for short, angry words or long waffly sentences and write down the effect they have.

Language Techniques in 'An Inspector Calls'

Priestley's a clever cookie — he uses techniques like dramatic irony to make his writing even better. You can be a clever cookie too — talk about dramatic irony in the exam to make your essays even better...

Priestley uses **dramatic irony**

1) In the play, it seems as if the Inspector knows everything. Priestley gives a similar power to the audience.
2) He set the play in 1912, but the play was first performed in 1945. So when Birling says that the *Titanic* is "unsinkable" the audience knows that Birling is wrong. It suggests he could be wrong about other things too, like thinking that social responsibility is "nonsense".
3) When the audience knows more than the characters, it's called dramatic irony.

The Birlings use **language** to **hide** what they **mean**

1) The Birlings avoid saying unpleasant things by using more acceptable words to hide what they mean.

- Gerald visits a bar which is a favourite place of the "women of the town" — a phrase used to refer to prostitutes. This hints that he's been paying for sex.
- Mrs Birling calls Eva/Daisy a "girl of that sort" — she means she is working class.
- Mr Birling says that Eva/Daisy was in a particular "condition" — he means she was pregnant.

2) The Inspector doesn't hide what he means — his language is more direct.

The Inspector uses colourful **imagery**

1) The Inspector uses horrible imagery to shock — the words "Burnt her inside out" create an image that upsets Sheila and the audience.
2) To emphasise the morality of his message, the Inspector uses imagery from the Bible in his final speech:

- The idea that "We are members of one body" is found in the Bible.
- The words "fire and blood and anguish" sound like the words used to describe the end of the world in the Book of Revelation.

The Inspector upsets Sheila with his harsh language.

Dramatic irony — more effective than dramatic ironing...

It's sometimes easy to get caught up in the action of the play, but Priestley has carefully chosen his language and imagery — don't forget to look at his techniques as well as what the characters do.

Practice Questions

So, you've thought about the way the play looks and sounds on stage — now try your hand at some of these quick questions. Don't spend too much time answering them — and if you can't remember the answer, go back through this section to remind yourself.

Quick Questions

Q1 What is the effect of having a small set for the play?

Q2 Give an example of a stage direction from the play that suggests that Eric is drunk.

Q3 How does the lighting change in the play?

Q4 The Birlings all start off seated and well-behaved. How does this change over the course of the play?

Q5 Why does Priestley use cliffhangers at the ends of Acts?

Q6 Find two examples of language that reveal the Birlings' attitudes in the play.

Q7 Why does the Inspector use horrible imagery to describe Eva/Daisy's death?

Practice Questions

Right — bring on the big guns. It's likely that you'll need to show that you know about the writer's techniques in your exam. Even if the question doesn't mention it, it's good to show that you know *An Inspector Calls* is a play rather than just a story.

In-depth Questions

Q1 Quickly sketch a set layout for a new production of *An Inspector Calls*. Explain the effect your design is intended to create.

Q2 How does Sheila's change in language during the play affect your opinion of her?

Q3 If you were directing a production of *An Inspector Calls*, and decided to have Eva/Daisy on stage, what sort of costume would you choose for her? Explain your answer.

Exam-style Questions

Q1 Look again at the passage in Act One from "Sheila: What - what did this girl look like?" to "Inspector: Well, Miss Birling?"

How does Priestley make this such a dramatic and powerful moment in the play?

Think about:
- What the Inspector says and does
- The reaction of Sheila
- The reaction of Mr Birling

Q2 Discuss how the Inspector uses language differently to the other characters in the play.

Think about:
- What the Birlings say, and how they say it
- What the Inspector says, and how he says it

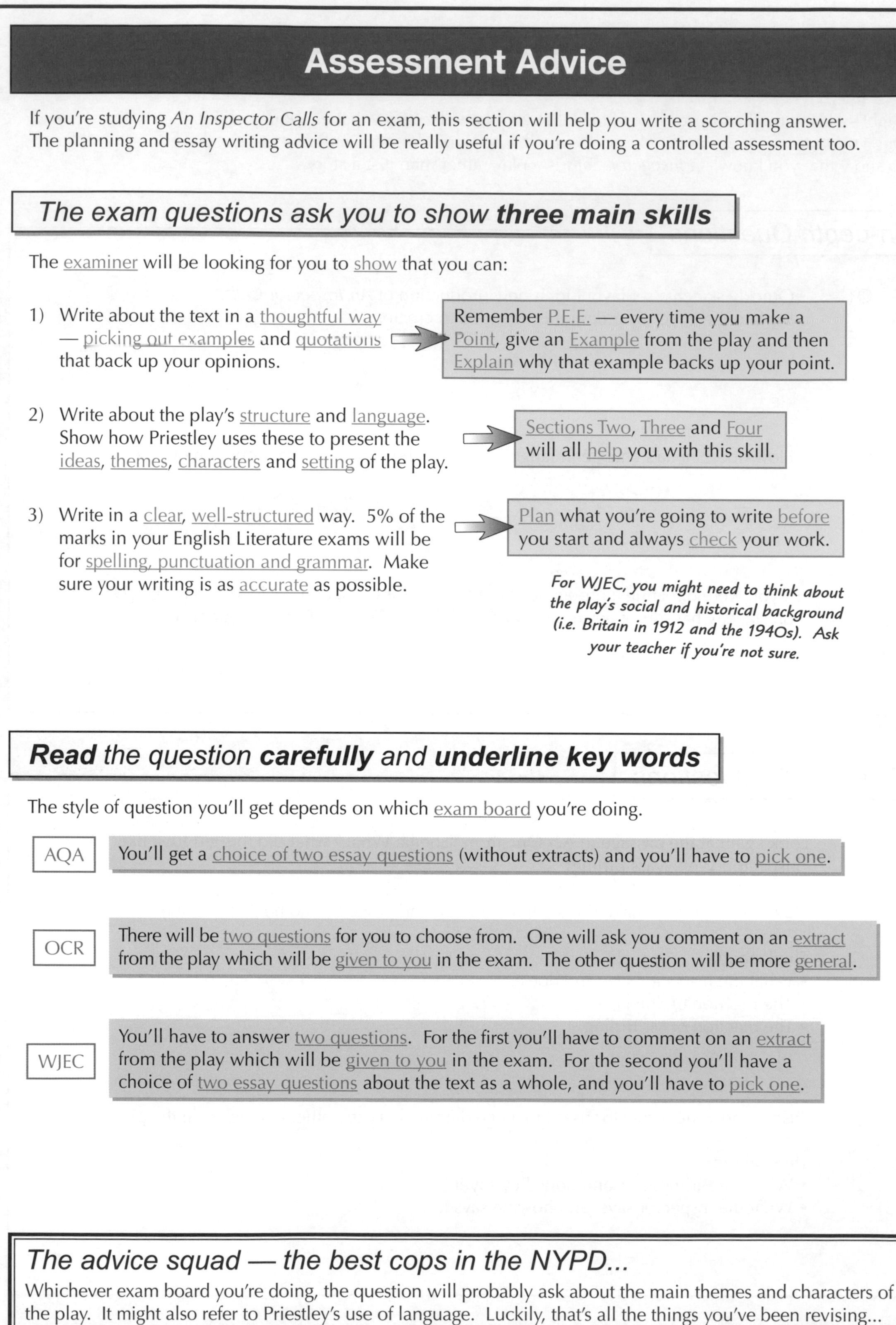

Assessment Advice

If you're studying *An Inspector Calls* for an exam, this section will help you write a scorching answer. The planning and essay writing advice will be really useful if you're doing a controlled assessment too.

The exam questions ask you to show ***three main skills***

The examiner will be looking for you to show that you can:

1) Write about the text in a thoughtful way — picking out examples and quotations that back up your opinions.

   Remember P.E.E. — every time you make a Point, give an Example from the play and then Explain why that example backs up your point.

2) Write about the play's structure and language. Show how Priestley uses these to present the ideas, themes, characters and setting of the play.

   Sections Two, Three and Four will all help you with this skill.

3) Write in a clear, well-structured way. 5% of the marks in your English Literature exams will be for spelling, punctuation and grammar. Make sure your writing is as accurate as possible.

   Plan what you're going to write before you start and always check your work.

For WJEC, you might need to think about the play's social and historical background (i.e. Britain in 1912 and the 1940s). Ask your teacher if you're not sure.

Read *the question* ***carefully*** *and* ***underline key words***

The style of question you'll get depends on which exam board you're doing.

AQA — You'll get a choice of two essay questions (without extracts) and you'll have to pick one.

OCR — There will be two questions for you to choose from. One will ask you comment on an extract from the play which will be given to you in the exam. The other question will be more general.

WJEC — You'll have to answer two questions. For the first you'll have to comment on an extract from the play which will be given to you in the exam. For the second you'll have a choice of two essay questions about the text as a whole, and you'll have to pick one.

The advice squad — the best cops in the NYPD...

Whichever exam board you're doing, the question will probably ask about the main themes and characters of the play. It might also refer to Priestley's use of language. Luckily, that's all the things you've been revising...

Structure and Planning

It's easy to panic in the exam — all the more reason to spend five minutes jotting down a cunning plan for what you're going to write before you start. Writing your plan down will help you stick to it and not waffle.

Plan your answer before you start

1) If you plan, you're less likely to forget something important.
2) Write your plan at the top of your answer booklet and draw a neat line through it when you've finished.
3) Don't spend too long on your plan. It's only rough work, so you don't need to write in full sentences. Here are a few examples of different ways you can plan your answer:

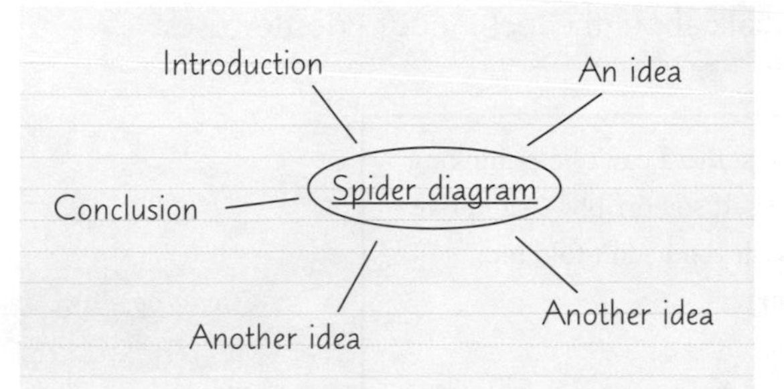

A point in a table...	Quote to back this up...
Another point...	Quote...
A different point...	Quote...

Bullet points and headings...
- Intro...
- An idea...
- The next idea...

Structure your answer

Start your essay with an introduction. It should be a short paragraph which outlines your main points in answer to the question.

The middle section of your essay should explain your answer in detail. Write a new paragraph for each point. Start by making your point, then back it up with an example (or a quotation). Then explain how the example backs up your point.

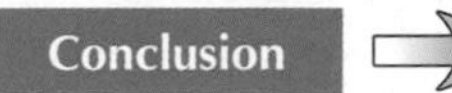

Remember to write a conclusion — a paragraph at the end which sums up your main points.

Try to use examples and quotes in your answer

Always back up your points with examples or quotes.

1) An example is when you describe a bit of the play to back up what you're saying.

   Sybil is a cruel character. For example, she persuades her charity not to help Daisy.

2) A quote is where you write down a word or a phrase from the actual play.

   Sybil is a cruel character. When Daisy asks Sybil's charity for help, Sybil uses her "influence to have it refused".

To plan or not to plan, that is the question...

The answer is yes, yes, a thousand times yes. Often people dive right in rather than making a plan. But 5 minutes spent organising a well-structured answer is loads better than pages of waffle. Mmm waffles...

Extract Question

For some exam boards you'll have to answer a question about an extract from *An Inspector Calls*. The next two pages will show you how to do this, but they'll still be useful if you don't have this type of question.

*Here's an **exam question** about an **extract** from the play*

1) Here's an exam question and extract. It's a good idea to pick out the key words from the question first.
2) It's also useful to highlight the important bits of the extract. Write down any ideas you have on the paper.

Q1 How does Priestley make this scene dramatic and powerful?

You only need to write about the extract. — You need to talk about the techniques Priestley uses.

SHEILA (*rather distressed*) Sorry! It's just that I can't help thinking about this girl — destroying herself so horribly — and I've been so happy tonight. Oh I wish you hadn't told me. What was she like? Quite young?

INSPECTOR Yes. Twenty-four.

SHEILA Pretty?

INSPECTOR She wasn't pretty when I saw her today, but she had been pretty — very pretty.

BIRLING That's enough of that.

GERALD And I don't really see that this inquiry gets you anywhere, Inspector. It's what happened to her since she left Mr Birling's works that is important.

BIRLING Obviously. I suggested that some time ago.

GERALD And we can't help you there because we don't know.

INSPECTOR (*slowly*) Are you sure you don't know.

He looks at GERALD, *then at* ERIC, *then at* SHEILA.

BIRLING Are you suggesting now that one of them knows something about this girl?

INSPECTOR Yes.

BIRLING You didn't come here just to see me then?

INSPECTOR No.

The other four exchange bewildered and perturbed glances.

BIRLING (*with marked change of tone*) Well, of course, if I'd known that earlier, I wouldn't have called you officious and talked about reporting you. You understand that, don't you, Inspector? I thought that — for some reason best known to yourself — you were making the most of this tiny bit of information I could give you. I'm sorry. This makes a difference. You sure of your facts?

INSPECTOR Some of them — yes.

BIRLING I can't think they can be of any great consequence.

INSPECTOR The girl's dead though.

SHEILA What do you mean by saying that? You talk as if we were responsible —

Stage directions show Sheila is emotional.

Strong, upsetting language to shock the audience.

Priestley makes Eva sound young and attractive so the audience feel sorry for her.

Language shows tension between the characters on the stage.

Hints the Inspector knows what happened. This increases tension.

Information is released bit by bit. This increases suspense.

Birling's tone becomes polite. This shows he's either relieved or worried.

Direct language. The Inspector gets to the point.

Hints at what will happen later.

Extract Question

When you've read the extract it's time to write your essay plan. And then the actual essay... If this seems like a lot to do in the time you've got, write a practice essay as part of your revision and time yourself.

Use your **notes** to make an **essay plan**

1) Here's an example of an essay plan you could write to answer the question on p.52.

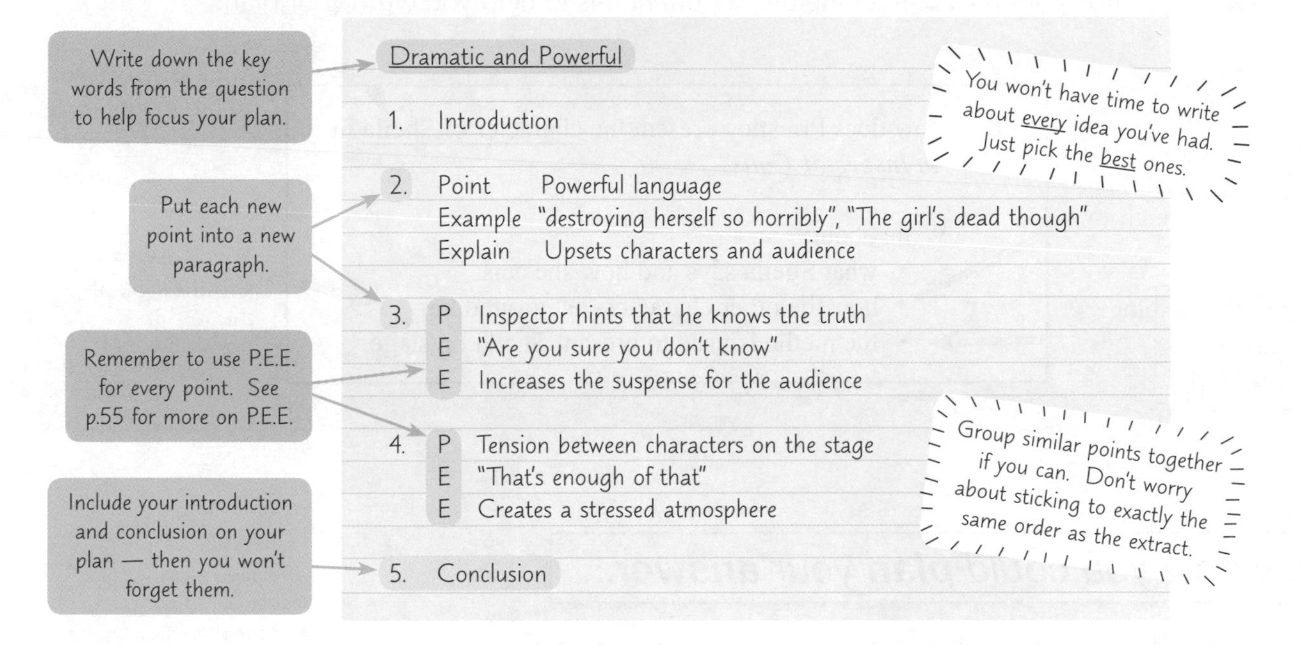

2) When you've finished writing your plan, read the question again.
3) Make sure every point in your plan answers the question.
4) You won't get any marks for points that don't have anything to do with the question.

Use your **plan** to write a **fantastic essay**

Here are some tips for writing a brilliant *An Inspector Calls* essay:

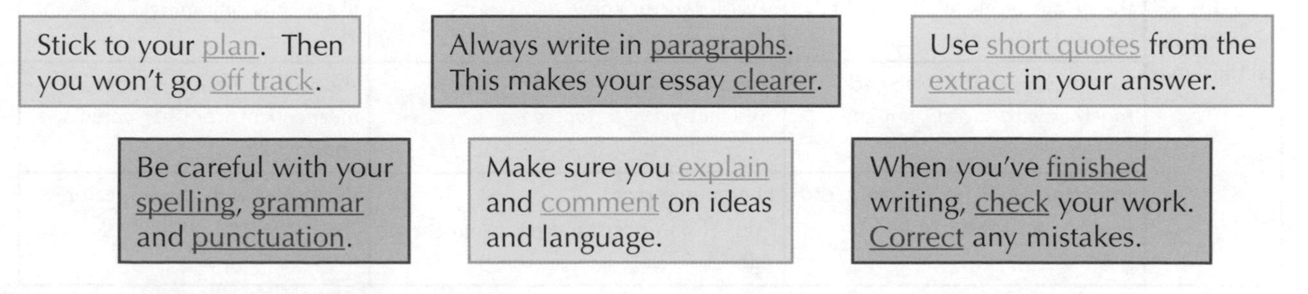

The best plan for your exam is... to plan

You're going on holiday. You haven't booked your flights or your hotel, but you think, 'I'm sure it'll be fine'. What a disaster that holiday was — I had a terrible time... That's the kind of mess you'll be in if you don't plan.

Sample Exam Question

Now it's time to have a look at an exam question without an extract. The next three pages contain loads of useful tips about how to write a fabulous exam answer, and a handy plan, table-style.

Here's a **sample exam question**

Read the exam question carefully. Underline the important bits to help you write your plan:

Q1 How does Priestley present the character of Sheila in *An Inspector Calls*?

Write about:
- what Sheila says and how she acts
- how the other characters act around her
- the methods used to present Sheila on stage

Remember to write about all the bullet points you're given.

Methods are things like stage directions and language.

Your answer's got to be about Sheila.

Your answer should look at the whole play.

Here's how you could **plan** your **answer...**

Keep looking back at the question to make sure you're answering it.
Here's an example plan for the question above:

If you're given bullet points in the question, remember to write about all of them — you'll lose marks if you don't.

	Point	method / example	explanation
What Sheila says and how she acts	starts out childish	stage directions "*rather excited*", "*playful*"	shows how young and carefree she is
	feels terrible for getting Eva/ Daisy sacked	emotional language and stage directions "I felt rotten about it" "*miserably*"	shows she has strong feelings of regret, unlike her parents
	grows up during the play — character that changes the most	direct language "I'm not a child"	suggests that there's hope for the future
How the other characters act around her	Gerald tries to protect her from the details of his affair but she refuses to leave the room	forceful language "I've a right to know"	she doesn't want to be treated like a child any more
	parents want her to get back together with Gerald but she refuses	direct language "No, not yet. It's too soon."	shows she's becoming more independent from her parents and Gerald
	Inspector treats her like an ally — they both want to find out the truth	honest language "Yes - I do understand her. And she's right".	she agrees with the Inspector that social responsibility is important

What do examiners eat? Why, egg-sam-wiches of course...

The most important thing to remember is DON'T PANIC. Take a deep breath, read the question, read it again, write a plan... take another deep breath... and then start writing. Leave about five minutes at the end to check your work too.

Worked Answer

So you've read the question a few times and you've written your plan... Next it's time to actually start writing your answer. Here's some wise advice that'll make it seem as easy as spotting an elephant in a field of sheep.

All answers should start with an *introduction*

1) Start your answer with a short introduction. → Say what you're going to talk about in the essay.
2) Here's an example of what you could write:

> This essay is about the character Sheila. Sheila is Mr and Mrs Birling's daughter. She's in her early twenties and is engaged to Gerald Croft. Most of the characters in the play treat her like a child because she acts like a little girl.

3) Everything in this introduction is true, but it doesn't answer the question — it's just a list of facts about Sheila.
4) Here's a better example:

> Priestley presents Sheila at the start of the play as childish and weak. She is controlled by the more powerful characters, like Gerald. But, by the end of the play, Priestley's language and stage directions show that she has grown up and has started to challenge her parents.

This bit says how the character of Sheila acts.

This bit says how the other characters act around her.

This bit mentions the methods that Priestley uses.

Start a *new paragraph* for each *new point* you make

1) Every time you make a new point, start a new paragraph.
2) Remember PEE:

Point	Make a point to answer the question you've been given.
Example	Give an example or a quote from the text which backs up your point.
Explain	Explain how the example or quote backs up the point you've made.

3) Here's an example of how to use PEE:

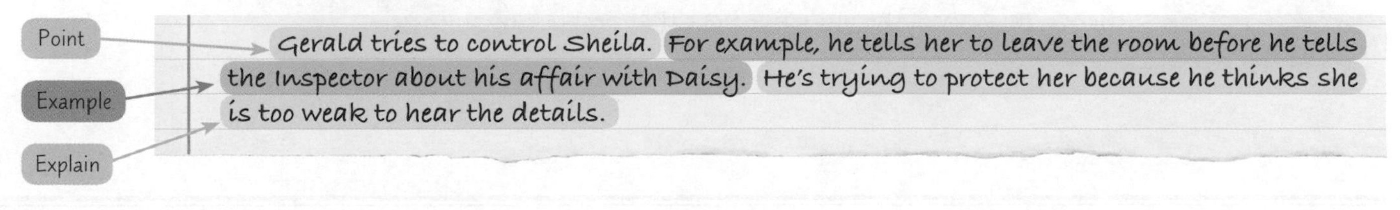

Gerald tries to control Sheila. For example, he tells her to leave the room before he tells the Inspector about his affair with Daisy. He's trying to protect her because he thinks she is too weak to hear the details.

Worked Answer

To really impress the examiner you've got to add a few snappy quotes to your answer. Even if you get to take the text into the exam it's a good idea to learn some short quotes so you don't spend too long reading.

Try to use **quotes** in your **answer**

See p.51 and p.55 for more advice on examples and quotes.

1) Use quotes to back up your point. Quotes don't have to be really long — just a few words is much better.

> Sheila refuses to leave because she wants to hear what Gerald has to say. She says, "I'm supposed to be engaged to Gerald. And I'm not a child, don't forget. I've a right to know." This shows that she is becoming more independent.

This quote is way too long.

2) Instead of copying whole sentences from the play, try to fit short quotes into your own sentence:

These quotes are quicker to copy out (and easier to remember).

> Sheila refuses to leave. She says, "I've a right to know". She even reminds Gerald that she is "not a child". This shows that she is not weak, like Gerald thinks, and is becoming more independent.

3) Try to memorise some key quotes so you can easily use them in an exam answer.
4) Start with one for each character and one for each theme.

Character — Birling

"hard-headed, practical man of business".

Theme — Social Responsibility

"We are members of one body. We are responsible for each other".

Leave yourself **time** to write a **conclusion**

1) Keep your eye on the clock and make sure you've got a bit of time left to write your conclusion.
2) Your conclusion should:
   - Sum up your reactions and feelings.
   - Give a really clear answer to the question.
3) Here's an example of what you could say:

Start a new paragraph for your conclusion.

You should include ideas about how an audience might react.

> In conclusion, Sheila's character changes over the course of the play. In the beginning, she's selfish and shallow, like her parents. When the Inspector calls, he teaches her a lot about morals and responsibility. By the end of the play she challenges her parents and stands up to them. This gives the audience hope that people can change.

Why do alligators write good essays? Because their quotes are snappy...

It seems like there's a lot to remember on these two pages, but there's not really. Write an introduction and conclusion, start a new paragraph for each new point you make, and remember Point, Example, Explain. Oh, and pop in some quotes.

Glossary

dramatic irony	When the audience knows something that the characters don't.	E.g. Birling says that the *Titanic* is "unsinkable", but we know it sank on its first journey.
hypocrite	Someone who says one thing but then does the opposite.	E.g. Gerald thinks that women should be protected from "unpleasant" things, but he did unpleasant things to Daisy.
imagery	Descriptive language that creates a picture in your mind.	E.g. "Burnt her inside out".
prejudice	Having a negative opinion about someone that's based on things like their social class, gender or background.	E.g. "As if a girl of that sort would ever refuse money!"
social responsibility	The idea that everyone is responsible for each other, and that one person's actions affect everybody else.	E.g. "We don't live alone. We are members of one body."
socialism	The idea that money and power should be shared more equally in society.	E.g. The Inspector thinks that the working class should be treated more fairly.
stereotype	Having an idea about a group of people before really knowing them e.g. women, working-class people.	E.g. Eric says all women are "potty" about clothes.
theme	An idea or topic that's important to a piece of writing.	E.g. Social class is an important theme in *An Inspector Calls*. The characters represent different social classes.

Index

The Characters from 'An Inspector Calls'

Phew! You should be an expert on *An Inspector Calls* by now. But if you want a bit of light relief and a quick recap of the play's plot, sit yourself down and read through *An Inspector Calls — The Cartoon*...

J. B. Priestley's 'An Inspector Calls'